Travelling with Resilience

Essays for Alastair Haggart

Scottish Episcopal Church
General Synod Office
21 Grosvenor Crescent
Edinburgh EH12 5EE

June 2002

ISBN   0 905573 54 4

Designed and typeset by the General Synod Office

Printed and bound by Mcgilvray Printers, Kirkcaldy

ALASTAIR IAIN MACDONALD HAGGART
1915 - 1998

For Mary, Alison, Mary Grace
and all who loved Alastair

Travellers

I think of the continent
of the mind. At some stage
in the crossing of it a traveller
rejoiced. This is the truth,
he cried; I have won
my salvation!

What was it like
to be alive then? Was it a time
when two sparrows were sold
for a farthing? What recipe
did he bequeath us for the solution
of our problems other than the statement
of his condition? The territory
has expanded since then. We
see now that the journey is
without end, and there is no joy
in the knowledge. Going on, going
back, standing aside – the alternatives
are appalling, as is the imagining
of the last traveller, what he would
say to us, if he were here
now, and how discredited we would find it.

Contents

Contributors

John Clarke: former student of Coates Hall: Principal, Ripon Theological College, Cuddesdon

Martin Conway: formerly President, Selly Oak Colleges, and Secretary to the Board of Ecumenical Affairs, B.C.C.

John Fitzsimmons: formerly Rector of the Scots College, Rome: Convener of The Unity, Faith & Order Commission of A.C.T.S.

John Habgood: formerly Archbishop of York: Chairman, Inter-Church Meeting 1985-1989

Michael Hare Duke: formerly Bishop of St. Andrews, Dunkeld and Dunblane: pastoral theologian

David Haslam: formerly Secretary, B.C.C. Community and Race Relations Unit

Richard Holloway: formerly Bishop of Edinburgh, Primus, Scottish Episcopal Church

ix

Michael Ingham: former student of Coates Hall, Bishop of New Westminster, Episcopal Church of Canada

Mary Tanner: ecumenical theologian: co-chair of A.R.C.I.C.: consultant to 1988 Lambeth Conference

Elizabeth Templeton: member of Division of Ecumenical Affairs, 1983-89: A.C.T.S. U.F.O. Commission: consultant to 1988 Lambeth Conference

Thomas F. Torrance: Emeritus Professor of Christian Dogmatics, University of Edinburgh: theologian and writer

Rowan Williams: Archbishop of Wales: theologian and writer: consultant to 1988 Lambeth Conference

Foreword

Kevin Franz

A foreword ought not to begin with a word of farewell. Yet there was a moment in the last conversation Alastair and I had in the ward of the Astley Ainslie Hospital in Edinburgh which had the character both of a summing-up and of an invitation. Alastair had been asleep when I arrived, but once awake he made a swift transition to alert engagement. It was a characteristic conversation, touching on family and parish life, the hospital's regime of care and also requiring me to give an account of what I had been reading. We were talking of our mutual regard for George Steiner when, with an emphasis both intellectual and deeply felt, Alastair said: 'Reality is greater than the facts'. It was a moment which given his physical frailty might have been simply poignant but was instead a moment of disclosure, even of communion.

The essays which are gathered together in this volume will, I hope, share in that character, disclosing the man, the subtle yet grounded nature of his faith, and, most significantly, the God in whom he believed and trusted.

If reality is greater than the facts, the facts themselves are nonetheless revelatory. As Elizabeth Templeton's opening memoir shows, the movement from Strathnaver to Edinburgh with all the places in between was not only a journey of resilience but one which honoured and gave space to each stage. Reading again of Alastair's roots within the Free Church I was reminded of one of the great poetic voices to emerge from Gaelic culture, Iain Crichton Smith.

In his poem 'Entering Your House' Crichton Smith captures

something of the narrowness of the tradition which made such a journey necessary:

> 'Entering your house, I sniff again
> the Free Church air, the pictures on the wall
> of ministers in collars, all these dull
> acres of brown paint, the chairs half seen
> in dim sad corners by the sacred hall
>
> under the spread antlers of that head
> mildly gazing above leathern tomes.
> So many draperies in so many rooms.
> So many coverlets on each heavy bed.
> A stagnant green perpetuates these glooms.
>
> And then the stairs. The ancient lamps and the
> scent of old prayers, texts of 'God is Love'.
> Did any children grow through all this grief?'

(From Collected Poems, Iain Crichton Smith (1992))

By contrast Alastair's own reflective piece on preaching, which closes this volume, expresses his delight in the sight of a young person's growing. His own unexpected ease of relationship with children was wonderfully demonstrated when he came on one occasion to admit two small boys to Communion in Wester Hailes. Uncharacteristically he had not prepared a sermon, but instead built a reflection on the conversation he had with the children when he arrived. When asked why he wanted to be part of this community one boy said simply, "Because I like it here."

The young Haggart's movement beyond the constraints of the Free Church had caused him some trepidation. Who could forget Alastair's account of his plucking up courage to confess to his family his impending movement even beyond the Church of Scotland and into the Anglican church? One elder responded thoughtfully: "I've aye thought they were fair riddled with Erastianism". Later it was with great glee that Alastair always added "And of course, you know, he was right."

Yet Alastair's origins had profoundly marked him with a keen sense of belonging to a particular people and place, a sharp eye for social exclusion, a fearlessness in naming things as they were and above all a profound passion for truth. Iain Crichton Smith again, in his poem 'Puritans':

'There was no curtain between them and fire..
That was great courage to have watched that fire,
not placing a screen before it as we do
with pictures, poems, landscapes, a great choir
of mounting voices which can drown the raw
hissing and spitting of flame with other fire.
That was great courage to have stayed as true
to truth as man can stay......'

(From *Collected Poems*, Iain Crichton Smith (1992))

And here there seems a strong connection with several of the essays which follow, not least with those which deal with the character of being a bishop. That staying true to truth led Alastair to search, and it is that image of the bishop as one who searches which concludes Michael Hare Duke's essay. He writes of the way in which an older model of the bishop as 'guardian of the truth' was akin to that of the dragon menacingly guarding the treasure store against theft. Today this is giving way to a new but no less serious vocation. Now the bishop's role is to be undertaken more in the character of one who acts as 'guarantor of an honest and truthful process of search, the servant of Truth that is not a hard-edged artefact but more like a developing relationship of love...'.

xiii

Key to that distinctive search for truth which the bishop undertakes is the willingness to learn and then, and only then, to teach. There was, Alastair said, no authority without authenticity.

Elizabeth Templeton discerns that the teaching ministry lay at the very heart of Alastair's own sense of vocation. Never afraid to teach, the bishop should never be afraid to learn. Some of the essays in this collection are eloquent expressions of this truth. The sermon preached by the then doyen of Scotland's theologians, Thomas Torrance, was an extraordinarily powerful ecumenical statement to all who were present that day in St. Mary's Cathedral in Edinburgh. It was also a fine example of Alastair's eagerness to offer an opportunity, at the heart of the most publicly significant liturgical event in his career for learning.

In fact, here the triple dynamic of pastor/teacher/preacher begins to emerge as a seamless exercise of ministry. In characteristic style, beginning with an explication of Latin grammar, Alastair's own essay on preaching demonstrates how vital the interaction between the three roles must be, of how the preacher's mind is quickened, refreshed and enriched by the pastoral task, of how it is the pastoral relationship which makes the general particular and binds the pastor and the community served by deep bonds of affection. The hands held out at the communion rail in St Paul's Cathedral, Dundee, revealed to Alastair the precise job they did within Dundee's mills and factories. Nobody who heard him speak of this could forget how he loved and learned from the lives of particular men and women.

That learning, that openness to the new, mediated through reading and human interaction, was given energy by Alastair's boundless curiosity. It was that quality of curiosity allied to a genuine attentiveness to the other person's story or insight which fuelled his discovery of new things and which was so much in evidence in his pastoral visits in the diocese of Edinburgh. In tenements in Gorgie, in high-rise flats in Wester Hailes, in the streets of Selkirk his encounters with people left a deep impression. They were never 'courtesy' visits from which nothing much was expected. They were rich examples of the reality of a bishop's pastoral oversight, an overseeing of the people and priest in that place, and I can't have been alone in feeling that he had learned and understood more in the course of one visit than I ever had.

That curiosity and questing for the truth which animated Alastair as a person of faith and as a bishop was yoked to a wider imperative. This led beyond the church narrowly defined, to an engagement with the wider church and the society it served. Elizabeth Templeton speaks of Alastair's contribution to the creation of a 'spaciousness' within the culture of the Scottish Episcopal Church, the formation of a community of belief greater than the sum of its parts. But this was allied to a broader vision of what the church was and what it was for. It is no accident that Alastair offered such strong and respected leadership within the Anglican Communion at a time of change. There is a sense in which that project is inevitably an unfinished one, and one which mirrors the experience within each Anglican province, the challenge of maintaining solidarity, preserving communion, in the face of huge named and recognised diversities. How that project is developed will be important not only for world-wide Anglicanism, but for the world church. How is 'spaciousness' to become a characteristic of the church's core ethos, not least as energy slips from the formal ecumenical movement and the demands of inter-faith dialogue assume greater and greater importance? In much of this Alastair seems clearly now to have been one of those who glimpsed the interrelatedness of these matters. Both the essays which address matters of interfaith relations and of racial justice, and John Fitzsimmons' consideration of one of the neuralgic points of Christian ecumenical dialogue, demonstrate the urgency which Alastair felt.

How quickly we move from the particular to the general and back again. How are the essays in this celebratory volume to be read? Following Alastair's own style, might I suggest, with a pencil in hand ready to annotate, to correct, and to share with others? (And possibly with a glass of malt at the elbow.)

If Alastair Haggart's life were a poem, a concept he would, I think, have laughed at, it would have for me the character of T.S. Eliot's judgement on Dante:

> 'The majority of poems one outgrows and outlives, as one outgrows and outlives the majority of human passions: [his] is one of those which one can only just hope to grow up to at the end of life.'

Introduction

Almost as soon as I had put pen to paper requesting information or reminiscences about Alastair Haggart, it was clear I was in trouble.

Enough poured in for several volumes: and with the mass of papers, commonplace books, extracts from journals and conference programmes which were part of Alastair's hoarded resources, there was obviously going to have to be a draconian selection made for a mere biographical preface.

Secondly, several of Alastair's oldest and truest friends were convinced that he would have scorned the whole project with the same fierce reticence that had vetoed any eulogy at his funeral service. Could the project be undertaken in a way which was not, in spirit, an act of culpable civil disobedience, or even the betrayal of a friend?

Thirdly, Alastair's standards were exacting. At least two of those approached for essays were overcome by various diffidences, either about being *au fait* enough with the topic, or about having enough theological sophistication to meet Alastair's posthumous gimlet-like brain. No coaxing could persuade them that this was false modesty. Even at the level of grammar and punctuation, one correspondent warned me, the eventual text must be 200% impeccable! Not a split infinitive or misplaced semi-colon should sully the publication!

Yet the invitation to honour his contribution to so many lives, to the Scottish Episcopal Church and the wider Anglican Communion, to the ecumenical life of Scotland and the wider U.K. and Irish scene seemed worth risking his wrath for. Though he had written, preached, conducted retreats and meditations on countless occasions, almost nothing was published: this too was part of his reticence, a reluctance to add to the overweight of publication he always deplored, finding much of it repetitive, derivative or dubiously worthwhile. Yet the fact that everything he wrote was 'occasional' belies the coherence of style and substance which was so convincingly palpable to those who knew him. In a culture where 'joined-up thinking' has become a mere political cliché, and where the churches seem on the edge of greater fragmentation and 'sectarianism' than for many decades, I hope this book serves as a reminder of the connectedness, the integrity of concerns which Alastair stood for.

Every contributor reflects some area of Alastair's multi-faceted interest in the life of church and world; not all would happily be theological bedfellows, but all were affirmed by Alastair as part of the vitality and energy of the ongoing journey to articulate faith and its implications.

Many more might have contributed. Most conspicuously, Lord Runcie's willingness to write something was overtaken, as the months passed, by his grappling with the effects of chemotherapy. My own underestimates of the editorial hiccoughs which are involved in such a compilation make me entirely answerable for the gap between dream and reality: by the time it was clear that Alastair's range of lay, secular and female friends and colleagues were underrepresented in the range of essays, it was too late to start recommissioning.

For compensation, my hope is that the biographical memoir not only indicates something of the range of Alastair's interests, but sets, in his own words, an agenda not to be lost sight of.

Some of the generously offered insights and memories were confidential: while, on the whole, there is no attempt here at 'intimate biography', I have usually not named individual sources *in situ*. All those named in the appendix helped, in a variety of ways, to make the memoir possible.

To them, to Mary for her warm and practical encouragement; to Richard Holloway as instigator of the project; to John Stuart, Pat McBryde and Mary Wilkinson of the General Synod Office I am wholeheartedly grateful. Thanks are due also to Shona Paterson of A.C.T.S., who was hugely instrumental in preparing the manuscript for printing and to Stewart and Ginny Graham for proof reading.

One of Alastair's heroes, Peter Medawar, wrote in his autobiographical 'Memoir of a Thinking Radish':-

"It is a common fault of biographies to devote hours of 'research' to verifying biographical details upon which nothing hangs."

If I have missed more vital details, *mea culpa*. If I have managed to reflect at all the sense of journeying which was for Alastair, the Christian adventure, my debt is to the scores of people who offered salient insights.

Elizabeth Templeton

Alastair Haggart: a memoir

October 10, 1915 – January 11, 1998

Elizabeth Templeton

Strathnaver, in north Sutherland, was the site of Patrick Sellar's first butchering. In 1814, 'The Year of the Burnings', began a brutal eviction programme, driving hundreds from the townships and pastures of the relatively fertile strath, burning their homes and clearing the ground for sheep.

This was Alastair's ancestral family homeland, to which he once returned as the oldest living male relative, to dig the grave of an aunt who had just died.

The folk-memory of the Clearances was one of the elements which accelerated the growth of the Free Church in the Highlands and Islands of Scotland in the decades after 1843. For outrage at the collusion of 'maintained' Church of Scotland clergy in the strategies of landlord and factor was as much part of the psyche of the Disruption as any theological difference. To come from Strathnaver was to have that consciousness in the bloodstream.

Though Alastair's parents moved south, via Fort William, to settle in Glasgow, his upbringing was in the Free Church tradition. Some journey, then, which saw him end up as Primus of the Scottish Episcopal Church (tainted also in much Scottish folk-consciousness as the church of the landowners).

What influences, apart from his own robust independence of thought and feeling, began his ecclesiastical journey are not

1

clear. The transition lies in a fairly shadowy period between his schooling in Hyndland Secondary School and his entry to Coates Hall as an ordinand in October of 1938.

He used to tell, playfully, of a Damascus-road holiday spent with his Sutherland aunt. Given permission to take a Sunday afternoon walk with his sister, he was warned that there was to be 'no playing'. (Swing parks in the Outer Hebrides are still tied up from Saturday night until Monday morning!) However, a haystack big enough to slide on proved irresistible, and Alastair was doomed enough to catch his arm on a projecting nail and return home bleeding. Confession was extracted. "It was," Alastair said, "The pleasure with which she applied the iodine which persuaded me that I must become an Episcopalian".

Several comments from much later in his life provide clues to what was probably not, demythologised, an on-the-spot decision, but the outcome of a process of wrestling and reflection in a serious young man for whom 'asking questions' was a life-long vocation.

In one of the many sermons to be preached during the 1984 Bicentennial Celebrations of Samuel Seabury's consecration in Aberdeen, he writes

> "I was brought up in a Church in which personal commitment to Christ was looked for. One of my great problems and distresses was that I could never identify with the experience of the people who bore witness to their understanding."
>
> (Hartford, Connecticut, 18.11.84)

The insistence of evangelical traditions on individual, internal certainty about Christ as personal saviour never rang true for

2

Alastair, who repeatedly affirmed, with provocative candour, that he had 'no faith of my own'. He was deeply suspicious of claims to special, particular religious experiences, and certainly unwilling to accept them as necessary or sufficient preconditions of true faith. Part of the spaciousness he came to feel in the Episcopal Church was that it made room for a more diffuse account of faith as belonging, practising, being a member of a community of belief which was greater than the sum of its parts.

If one element of his move was connected to his intellectual and emotional refusal to 'fake' a piety he could not share, another seems to have had more imaginative and aesthetic dimensions.

In a Christmas sermon preached on 'Beauty and Truth in Religion', he recalls a dialogue between Sebastian Flyte and Charles Ryder in *Brideshead Revisited*, where a sentence runs, "He feared that men's love of beauty would quench his love of truth". The whole thrust of the sermon is an appeal to resist the polarisation of truth and beauty, and to find both personal and corporate ways of living with the potential tension.

> "I was brought up in a church which, insofar as possible, excluded every appeal to the senses except that of hearing! There were no hymns, no organs, no decorations, flowers, crosses, pictures. The appeal was entirely through the spoken word."
>
> (Florida, 1994)

This rigorist position – 'the Word made flesh made word again' – he contrasts, with almost sixty years hindsight, with

> "The great Catholic tradition which has always

3

employed the senses is the expression of worship and belief, and used the senses as means through which belief can be conveyed, the senses of hearing, seeing, smelling, tasting and touching."

It is unlikely that the young confirmed Alastair who worshipped at St. Silas in Park Road, Glasgow, could at the time have glossed the use of incense as the sanctification of the sense of smell. (This was a low church evangelical congregation.) But some recognition of more expansive openness to the transcendent than strict Calvinist practice allowed, was an element in Alastair's more intuitive journeying.

Even in his new context, Alastair must have shown considerable independence of spirit, for St Silas was not, at that time, under the jurisdiction of the Scottish Episcopal Church, but owed its allegiance to the Bishop of Carlisle, who performed its confirmations. His decision to apply for ordination training to Coates Hall was seen by the congregation of St Silas as a serious error, and had to survive public intercession that he be guided to a less dangerous choice!

The decision about a vocation to priesthood lies untraceably in the years between the end of his schooling and his entry to Coates Hall in October 1938. Three years in North Wales with an engineering firm, and then a period with Burroughs Adding Machines as a salesman remain 'hidden years' even to Alastair's oldest friends. What is clear is that well back into the 30s, he had begun a life-long habit of keeping commonplace books, with a range of quotations which can hardly have been standard for adding machine salesmen; - Heloise and Abelard, John Stuart Mill, John Wesley, Francis de Sales, Thomas Browne, Julian of Norwich. (to take a sample from a few pages at random.)

This magpie interest in raiding and retaining gems of political, social and theological comment survived a lifetime, both in the form of commonplace books with extracts ranging from single aphorisms and epigrams to pages of copied text in minuscule handwriting, and, later, in the careful annotation in the back flycovers of books: pages noted for future reference and subject annotations, carefully cross-referenced.

Arrival at Coates Hall marks the first publicly attestable stage of his formation. Both James Robertson and Hugh McIntosh, whose friendship goes back to those days, have lively memories of this serious, bookish, somewhat reserved student, not much inclined to sport or light recreation, disciplined and fastidious in his ways, and intellectually avid. (James Robertson attests to Alastair's accepting his invitation to an afternoon walk on Corstorphine Hill, but only on condition that they discussed Christological heresies!)

The key influence on his development at this stage seems to have been the Coates Hall chaplain, David Borland, a well-read, musical, deeply cultured young man with a sense of the largesse of Europe's spiritual heritage. Alastair accompanied him on a visit to Oxford where he had his first meeting with the already legendary Donald MacKinnon, whose omnivorous intelligence and political engagement were both harnessed to a deeply sacramental Anglicanism. He also spent several weeks of the summer of 1939 at a reading party in Glen Urquhart organised by Borland, where a rich mix of physical exercise, intellectual exploration and good companionship could be experienced in a less cloistered setting than Coates Hall.

It takes historical imagination to reconstruct the severity and austerity of seminary training in the late 30s and early 40s. The day was regimented for prayer and study from early morning till ten at night, with only one hour of weekday recreation for the last hour before ten. The discipline was quasi-monastic, with compulsory overnight silence. The one or two married ordinands had no contact with their wives for most of the week, and neither wife nor girlfriend crossed the Coates Hall threshold. The kind of mixed, mobile, modular community reflected in John Clarke's essay in this volume seems to belong to another planet.

Alastair's academic gifts, albeit without the formal credentials of an Arts degree, meant that he was enrolled for the L.Th. course at Durham University, rather than for the General Ordination Examination. He enrolled at Durham to satisfy the residential requirement for the Licentiate in 1941, commuting it a year later to a B.A. degree, and then, during his curacy at Glasgow to an M.A. Had it not been wartime, the possibility of going on to do doctoral work might have beckoned. As it was, his determination to be deaconed in 1941 and ordained priest in 1942 in St. Mary's Cathedral Glasgow took priority. One of his peers speculates that being firmly in clerical orders saved him from painful decisions about non-combatant war service. His political convictions at this stage were left wing and pacifist. Horror at the Spanish Civil War, with its million casualties and its anticipation of Europe's coming nightmare made him a signatory of the Peace Pledge Union, though out-and-out pacifism seemed to him later to be too ideological a stance to be universalised.

Coates Hall had brought him out of his shell, as a fellow history student from Hatfield College, Walter Stranz, documents. Alastair was active in the Labour Club and in Student Union politics, as well as being a vocal advocate of the Student Christian Movement in Durham with its lively engagement in social, political and religious issues of the day. He was also actively disgruntled at the inadequacies of his lodgings in

Stalag 42, the house in which he had rooms during his year of study. Asceticism had its limits.

The commonplace book entries for 1941-42 show continuing catholicity of theological reading, much poetry (Blake, Hopkins, Housman) as well as extracts from the 'New Statesman', Joad, Huxley, and Russell. The taste for witty and economic asperity emerges in the often unattributed epigrams: 'a celibate is a man who thinks that the only marriage which was justified was the one which produced him', 'the only way to Hell is to be content to let others go there', 'he was no gentleman – he lived within his income'.

When he was back in Scotland, the key influence in these early years on Alastair's ministry was John (Jock) Murray, who was, by 1941, a priest of sixteen year's standing, and Provost of St. Mary's Episcopal Cathedral in Glasgow. Astute, capable, diligent and reputedly fierce enough with curates for Coates Hall to be full of commiserations when Alastair was sent to him, Murray clearly modelled for Alastair the character of priesthood. Appreciation was mutual, and for his second curacy Alastair followed Murray to Hendon, St. Mary's in North London, a church with long Anglo-Catholic roots and a history going back to mediaeval times.

Murray himself had been an altar-boy in Old St. Paul's, Edinburgh, in the 20s, and when he was preparing for ordination, the elderly women of the congregation, with special permission from the Royal Mint, had a set of communion silver (just big enough for weekday communions) made for him out of their gathered collection of silver groats and threepenny pieces. It was a potent symbol of a very personal 'apostolic succession' that Jock before his death passed this chalice and paten to Alastair and he in turn used it throughout his ministry, before returning it to Old St. Paul's in December, 1989.

Alastair, too, had attended Old St. Paul's as a Coates Hall student, and by the time he was ordained had moved some way from his St Silas evangelical low church tradition towards a more Anglo-Catholic understanding of liturgy, of the Christian Year, and of the Communion of the Saints. That sense of catholicity defined his preferred churchmanship, though never in florid or fundamentalist modes; and always in conjunction with a cool, liberal, intellectual temper informed by critical biblical and historical scholarship and by appreciation of the broad liberal sanity of men like Hensley Henson, William Temple and Michael Ramsey.

The decision to follow Jock Murray to Hendon, as well as being a sign of his personal loyalty, reflected an interest in gaining experience outside of Scotland which would consolidate some of the enrichment of his Durham time.

A lively account of his arrival comes from Paul Singleton, appointed at almost the same time as priest in charge of the daughter parish of St. Mary Magdalene's, Holden Hill, a bachelor priest who had moved into his parsonage early in 1946. He had heard from Jock Murray's wife intimidating accounts of this 'wonderful priest, brilliant scholar' who was joining the Hendon parish team, and was deeply alarmed one afternoon when the doorbell rang and he found on his doorstep "a tall young priest in a black coat … looking at me rather severely down a longish nose."

The encounter proceeded with some caution till Alastair responded to the tentative offer of a beer at the unhallowed hour of 5.30 with a detected note of relief that it was not too early for him. Within the hour, each discovered that the other had been dreading the meeting because of the panegyrics of Marjorie Murray. Relieved laughter generated a lifelong friendship.

Newly-married, Alastair and Peggy (née Margaret Trundle) must have struggled on a curate's salary in post-war North London. Walter Stranz recalls their ingenuity in constructing a sofa in their semi-detached terraced house, from a discarded car seat. Peggy had been a member of the St Mary's Cathedral congregation, a secretary by training. They had courted discreetly, out of the eyes of the parish, by virtue of bus or train excursions to Balloch on Loch Lomond. By all accounts Peggy, though somewhat in awe of her husband's intellectual prowess, was, in those days, a merry and vivacious young woman, untouched by the shadow of later recurrent depression which was to sap her vitality.

Role models for clergy wives were undisputed in those days. They made do with the time available when their husbands' work was done: and for an earnest and dedicated young priest one can only guess that that may not have meant a huge amount of time for recreation and domestic conviviality. Even much later, when the children were growing up - and family holidays were certainly sacrosanct by the late fifties - Peggy confided to a close friend that for Alastair, holidays meant two suitcases, the larger one being full of books!

With Jock Murray as advocate and mentor, Alastair's reputation back in Scotland was already growing. The Hendon parish magazine of April '48 announces his appointment, to take effect from 30th June, as Precentor of St. Ninian's, Perth. Murray writes:

> "It was exceedingly charitable of me to be as nice as I was to a receiving Northern Bishop descending on our ewe lambs and snatching him away …. His three years at Hendon will have given him, I hope, some width of experience which will make him much more competent in the ministry which he takes back to Scotland."

9

The next three years were spent in the third of the four Scottish dioceses in which Alastair learned his craft. Perthshire, then as now, both for the Episcopal Church and for the Church of Scotland was the heartland of gentrified Scotland, and must have presented some challenges to a socially and politically left-inclined young priest. Michael Hare Duke documents one remembered encounter when a local industrialist offered the gift of a car to make parish visiting easier. Alastair's documented, grave reply was:

> "I am extremely grateful for your generosity, but until your workers are paid more than a poverty wage, I do not believe that it would be right for a Christian minister to benefit from the profits of your company."

(One might contrast this response with that of George Macleod when challenged with the wickedness of accepting donations for Iona from wealthy capitalists: "I am willing to take anyone's dirty money and clean it for them!").

Certainly 'austerity' is a word which recurs in documentation from many who were part of Alastair's congregations in the 50s and 60s, and though there are glimpses of conviviality, and testimonies to immense pastoral understanding from every stage of his ministry, the mellow and urbane Alastair who emerged in his fifties and sixties represents some kind of gradual metamorphosis from this somewhat stern and authoritarian and professionally self-conscious younger man.

His first and only rectorship in St. Oswald's, Kings Park, from 1951-59, is vividly remembered by many of the key members of his parish. One documents an impression of battle between the incumbent warden "who believed it was part of his duty to let the new Rector know how things were done in St. Oswald's" and the new Rector who "believed equally sincerely it was his duty to let us know how things ought to be done in St. Oswald's". Another remembers an occasion when, in the middle of a dispute with the Vestry which was going against him, Alastair sent them into the cold church to pray about the matter, and was vindicated by having them come back, with one exception, converted to his position. His gifts of pragmatic compromise and his commitment to collegial decision-making had clearly not developed to the full at this stage! (Even when they had, however, he had no doubt that leadership was leadership, qualified but not negated by any such adjective as collegial. The buck stopped with him, and he had no time for indecisive shilly-shallying.)

Most of his energy and some of his intransigence was fired by a vision of a church of real vitality, nourishing its members and capable of convincing witness and challenge to the surrounding world. This centred for him on two things; the sharing in animated eucharistic life and the nourishment in understanding which could grow through preaching, teaching and learning in which clergy and people shared.

For all that there were strenuous ecumenical moves afoot via the Iona Community and the Scottish Churches Council, Alastair's central identity up to this point was clearly inside the Scottish Episcopal Church and its disciplines. He was a rigorist about admitting divorced persons to communion, and seems to have observed the canons which forbade eucharistic hospitality to or from non-Episcopalians with no sense of internal chafing. (Only in the late 60s, when exploratory permissive legislation was being mooted, did he invite Norman Orr, the Church of Scotland University Chaplain in Dundee, to communicate in St. Paul's).

It is hard to reconcile such memories, on paper sounding unbending and inflexible, with the other, equally well documented accounts of boyish vitality, fun and mischievous humour. Many, especially women, registered the somewhat forbidding exterior as a kind of professional cover for a man of considerable charm, humour, warmth and deeply private feeling. Those who worked with young people in his various charges testify to an easy and teasing rapport with youngsters, especially with the youth fellowships in Kings Park and the choristers in St. Paul's. He inspired his Sunday-school teachers, taking an active part in their weekly lesson preparation, which often evolved into late night discussions of their own far-ranging topics of theological interest.

With his own daughters, Alison and Mary Grace, he expected well-behaved habits of church-going, and insisted on the setting aside of reading time as a vital contribution to their intellectual nurture. But several stories suggest that he had a rueful appreciation of being outmanoeuvred. Robin Forrest, one of his ordinands in Kings Park, recalls Alastair trying three times to curb the noise level in the rectory as the children played with their friends one Saturday morning while he was working in his study. As he returned to work, he overheard Mary Grace saying to her friends "What do you do when your father gives you a telling off? I just hang my head and pretend to listen."

While at Kings Park, his workload was increased by an extension ministry as 'priest-in-charge' at St.Martin's, Glasgow from 1953 till 1958; and from 1958 to 1959 he was appointed Synod Clerk to the Glasgow Diocese, and Canon of St. Mary's Cathedral, opening up for him the experience of wider diocesan issues. That, on top of routine weekday services at 7am to let people attend before work, evening groups on several evenings a week for different constituencies, and the management of a congregation which he had inherited in a state of fairly slack routine was a punishing schedule. Those who worked with him registered that he asked nothing of others that he did not demand of himself: and his genuine concern about all aspect's of the church's life, from details of finance and fabric to intellectual and spiritual nurture made an impact which impressed and enthused many. At the same time, once he came to know and trust people as capable of taking responsibility for specific tasks, he willingly left them to get on with things. His gifts for talent-spotting and his huge interest in the welfare of people in his care generated a trust and warmth which counterpoised the sense of rigour and somewhat autocratic aloofness.

During his time at Kings Park he graduated from a Vespa scooter, on which he scooted around with his cassock kilted round his waist, to his first car, donated this time without the political taint of the earlier Perthshire offer. His insatiable curiosity involved spending several Saturday afternoons stripping down the engine and having a quick DIY introduction to motor mechanics.

It was, however, his next move, to be Provost of St. Paul's Cathedral, Dundee, which established him as a significant and prominent figure in the Episcopal Church landscape.

His parish newsletters, from his arrival in 1959 till his departure twelve years later, document his commitment to turning around an ailing and somewhat demotivated congregation, almost on the edge of financial bankruptcy, and not in good spiritual health.

The tone of his pastoral letters to his 'dear family' in the early 60s is fairly astringent.

"On any ordinary Sunday, over all the services, only about 25% of the congregation comes to worship God

.... I cannot believe that all the 75% who are absent are *reasonably* hindered. They are 'members of St. Paul's' only in the sense that they will expect me to marry them, or to baptise their babies, or, at the last, to bury them."

"Shall I tell you what you are? Lazy. The Devil ... encourages us to accept in a lazy, hazy kind of way, the Truth of the Christian Faith, but also to imagine that it doesn't really matter very much."

"You're a nice lot, but I suspect that if I didn't stick a pin in you from time to time, you'd mostly become a very dull lot."

Few priests would risk taking that tone with their congregations, but the approach seems to have paid off. The congregation's liturgical and eucharistic life was transformed: the music was overhauled, especially after the arrival of Robert Lightband the new organist. Before his arrival, Alastair had forbidden a choral anthem more than once a month, a restriction which he relaxed as the choir improved under its new direction. Things were put on a sound financial footing. Several significant posts of Diocesan responsibility were undertaken by Cathedral laymen such as Mr (later Sir) Lewis Robertson who was Diocesan Auditor, Professor Matheson, Master of Queen's College, who acted as Diocesan Chancellor and Professor McDonald of St. Andrew's Law Faculty who became Diocesan Registrar.

The association between men of such manifest capacity in public life and the affairs of the church was, to Alastair, a much appreciated symbol of the fact that Christianity was no matter of private pietism, but something capable of attracting and challenging the best minds of secular professionals. To some, this interest in encouraging people of such stature smacked of intellectual if not social elitism: but Alastair was equally appreciative of the widows' mites which came from modest members of the congregation who made contributions to beautifying the Cathedral fabric, or to helping with the crèche in summer. Above all, he prized the disciplined attendance at Sunday worship and the commitment to a few dedicated minutes of morning and evening prayer.

With his curates he could be fierce. One remembers Alastair fiddling with the Cathedral's loud speaker system while the curate preached at a Sunday morning service. Confronted by an angry curate at the end, with the words "you absolutely mangled my sermon!" Alastair's chilly reply was "It deserved to be mangled". He was punctilious about the spacing of candles, the dignity of liturgical procession, the polish on clerical shoes. Nothing scruffy or casual or slovenly was acceptable. Yet again, people seemed to recognise that he asked nothing of others which he did not demand of himself. He gladly took his turn in cleaning up spilled wax from candles, in offering double early morning communion which might allow people to come before work on Feast Days or during Holy Week.

Above all, he sought the creation of an 'informed, thoughtful, articulate Christian people', and devoted himself to that task. The clergy team could not, he believed, nourish people unless they maintained their own intellectual servicing as well as their devotional integrity, and weekly clergy meetings always involved an hour of tough study as well as matters of administration and strategy. Sermons were preached which exposed the congregation to the complexities of modern theological debate, cultural traits and the need for reflective responses to the questions thrown up by both. It was his conviction for over fifty years of preaching in all kinds of contexts, that if you preached up to people rather than down to them, they were capable of response, and furthermore of interest and enjoyment. As he put it in his farewell sermon in Dundee on Easter Day, 1971:-

"The intellect is a standard piece of human equipment, like the nose"

Both his preached sermons and his pastoral letters often introduced people to snippets from his reading, encouragement to try certain books, introductions to explore ideas: but the pitch was never ostentatiously scholarly. He didn't throw names around, or bamboozle people with technical jargon. Rather he invited them to unpack the meaning of phrases they took for granted, about judgement, or second coming, or the incarnation, deeply embedded in the liturgical vocabulary, but rarely explored. Teaching was at the core of his sense of vocation.

The sixties were, for church and culture, a time of turbulence. The range of social issues and concerns addressed in sermons and Cathedral activities was wide: the insights of contemporary psychiatry and psychology: urban poverty, exemplified in the work of the Gorbals Group: racism in British society: awareness of Third World issues: eye donation after death: the apartheid issue in South Africa.

Alastair put to a congregational meeting the question of whether people wanted him to address such issues from the pulpit, and was delighted when he was given a unanimous mandate to relate his preaching to contemporary events and problems. This he formulated as taking the 'alleged risk' of taking politics into the pulpit rather than committing the 'known sin of appalling silence'.

Experiment, with the positioning of altars, the liturgical responses, various postures for worship, the moving of communion rails, courses of sermons, ecumenical exploration of the limits of co-existence was to be conducted, in a distinctively Alastair-like phrase, 'with resilient caution'. Two principles governed the caution end: that nothing irreversible should be done which could not be undone if it turned out not to be helpful or creative: and that nothing should be done which committed the Cathedral to financial expense, struggling as it was to get its finances back on an even keel.

The resilience had deeper and less pragmatic roots. It came from the conviction that to be open to new possibilities was the only way of testing truth. He was utterly convinced of Newman's dictum that "here below, to live is to grow, to grow is to change, and to be perfect is to change often". While he had little enthusiasm for what he called '*Corybantic* Christianity' – enthusiastic charismatic piety – he was profoundly convinced that the presence of the Spirit in the church meant that there had to be ever open exploration of new and emerging questions; theological, ethical, ecclesiological and pastoral.

Working towards the creation of a 'flexible openness' was nothing to do with zeitgeist trendiness. It was based on the conviction that the Gospel was about the 'Christification of creation', and that one must therefore be *alert* for the presence of God at any point of historical or cultural development.

The sixties saw a huge acceleration in ecumenical activity and liturgical reform. The ripples of Vatican II touched many other ecclesiastical shores. The 'New Theologies' of Bultmann, Tillich and Bonhoeffer began to be widely accessible beyond the groves of academe. The sense of the global Anglican communion was beginning to develop under Michael Ramsey. (John Sprott, Bishop of Brechin comes back

17

from a 1962 visit to Lambeth Palace charged with a sense of Anglican involvement in world-wide concerns and ecumenical developments.) At the same time, events like the Nottingham Faith and Order Conference of 1964 were charting the processes of secularisation and seeming alienation between the church and the fields of contemporary knowledge and truth won by thinkers like Darwin, Freud and Marx and their successors.

In such a context, Alastair believed that peddling 'fraudulent certainty' was a failure of Christian nerve, a refusal to recognise that the Holy Spirit "seems to be a dab hand at taking risks".

He did not, on the other hand trust heady and premature radicalism which went faster than "the corporate mind of our Church". Exploring the question of change and continuity in his Easter parish letter of 1965 he writes of himself:

> "I am myself a bifurcated man. I am too old to be wholly on the side of the radicals, and not quite old enough to be at ease among the conservatives."

It was not, however, a question of age. If anything, he became more questioning and exploratory and radical as he got older. It was a matter of temperament and statesmanship, and conviction that catholicity could not be manifested by the absolutising of any single strand of doctrine or practice.

On the personal and domestic level, Peggy's illness intensified, at times requiring hospitalisation, and increasingly subjecting her to the side-effects of debilitating medication. Alastair tried very hard to separate family concerns and public congregational ones, but could hardly sustain that. When for about five months in 1963 Peggy was in hospital, he himself succumbed to pneumonia and his eighty year old mother moved in to look after the girls while he convalesced. In the July/August newsletter of that year he acknowledges reproaches from members of the congregation to the effect that 'The only members of the congregation who are not members of the Cathedral Family are the Provost's family'. Recognising his personal distaste for 'writing about ourselves in the magazine', he registers appreciation of the sympathy and prayerful concern of the congregation with the telling sentence: 'It is rather wonderful to feel that you "belong".' He is similarly touched by the expression of congregational goodwill on the occasion of his daughter Alison's wedding in October 1968, and by the recognition of his own silver wedding on May 14th, 1970. Learning to let himself be receiver as well as giver, visibly human as well as capably professional seems to have been part of the mellowing process.

Shortly after being awarded an honorary LL.D. by Dundee University for services to the community, he was invited by the College of Bishops to accept the Principalship of Coates Hall. While it was clearly a wrench to leave a congregation he had so nourished and grown with, the job prospect filled him with elation.

"To be paid to read, to think and to teach – all this and heaven too."

The four years of his principalship transformed Coates Hall. While the commitment to specific Episcopal seminary training remained, the atmosphere of the College was galvanised by his intellectual and cultural commitments. During the early 70s, he attracted to Coates Hall students of high intellectual calibre, and forged stronger links with the Theological Faculty in New College than had existed before, offering the main theological training to ordinands who had entrance qualifications for the B.D. degree, and combined their priestly formation with four days a week of attendance at university courses.

The seminary aspect of life in Coates Hall was clearly modified by the fact that the bulk of the students were out and about in the public life of the university for over half the time , but Alastair also took their specific ecclesiastical training with great seriousness and rigour. The highest standards of punctuality and preparation for worship leadership were expected. Constitutionally, Alastair was incapable of understanding laziness, and certainly had no sympathy for things done slothfully or with slovenliness.

Yet he also relished a relationship with his students which was not at all distant or remote; one of affection and at times playfulness, and of unfailing attentiveness to the detail which would make things work – like regularly visiting a Reformed Church Indonesian Ph.D. student who lived in Coates Hall for two years, coping with the double culture shock of Scottish climate and Episcopalian liturgy.

The staff team, with Donald Guthrie and Kenneth Strachan, was a strong one. Kenneth's shrewd, dry, pawky Scots wit and wide generous humanity in particular were immensely important to Alistair: no trace of pretentiousness or pomposity could survive the scrutiny of Kenneth's sturdy anti-clericalism. When, many years later, Alastair conducted Kenneth's funeral service, one could almost see the twinkle behind the gravity as the assembled bishops were invited to sit in the pews, unrobed, with the ordinary congregation they belonged to!

The all too brief four years in Coates Hall are judged by many of Alastair's friends to have marked a considerable mellowing. An environment of committed and lively young men, willing to engage in debate and even rebellion with the 'Prin': the chance to invite a huge range of theological and secular speakers to enrich the life of the college: the grace of being teased for the piles of books which would accompany him when he preached: the opportunity to shape the sense of vocation for many who would themselves rise to positions of influence and responsibility: in orchestrating and overseeing all this, he was in his element.

"Teach, teach, teach" was his constant exhortation to the students, since he never believed that sacerdotal functions exhausted ministry. To be a teaching pastor, enabling ordinary people to reflect on the huge questions arising from traditional faith's dialogue with modernity, was central for him to the priestly commitment. Nothing offended him so much as having former students, who should have known better, preaching as if they were fundamentalists. From a few this elicited resentment; they regarded his relentless intellectualism as a kind of elitism, and disagreed with his rooted conviction that congregations responded best to being stretched from the pulpit. But for Alastair, "Ignorance had no rights", at least not if it was born of inertia, fear, or a phoney paternalistic protectionism.

Alastair's agenda was to make connections, and it is no accident that he developed a cordial friendship with Leslie Houlden, then Principal at Cuddesdon at Oxford, and equally committed to the integration of faith and scholarship which was so central to the classic liberal motivation. Awareness, not only of biblical and theological developments, but of discoveries in psychiatry, sociology, cosmology, medicine, had to be taken on board and wrestled with, for truth could not properly be compartmentalised. Martin Conway's sermon, included in this volume, would have appealed to him!

Despite his proven abilities, or perhaps because of them – ecclesiastical jealousies being what they are – Alastair had been an episcopal candidate for several Dioceses before he was elected, at the age of 60, as Bishop of Edinburgh. In this instance, he won overwhelmingly, and, though it must have been some wrench to give up his loved job in the theological college, he had no false modesty about his ability to tackle the task. The advice of Kenneth Woolcombe, Bishop of Oxford, had been "Alastair, *enjoy* being a Bishop!" and Alastair was resolved to endorse the sentiment. "God has little use for sorry saints and still less for doleful bishops" he said in his installation sermon.

Knowing himself as a temperamental pessimist, he nevertheless felt sustained and encouraged by the warmth and loyalty expressed by countless friends; and 'the proper lightness of spirit' wished for him and Peggy by Sir Lewis Robertson was not, in fact, swamped by the largeness of the task.

As ever, he set about the work methodically and with realism and foresight.

As *pastor pastorum*, he took Episcopal visitation seriously, aiming to visit each congregation in the Diocese once every two years. This he sustained even after his election as Primus in 1977 added a whole raft of new responsibilities within the Anglican Communion to his existing ones. He would usually stay a couple of days in each charge, asking for the hospitality of the Rectory household if he was out of Edinburgh, eager to suss out both the needs of the clergy and their wives and families, the health of the congregation and the state of the wider community.

Characteristically, he would send a memo ahead of time:

"Please will you let me know when you expect me to arrive and give me some idea of what you expect me to do (Services? Preachments? Meetings? Vestry? Congregation? Community?) Don't hesitate about planning a full day!"

He felt this as a genuine enrichment of his ministry, helping him to understand better and respond more practically to the opportunities and needs experienced by the clergy and laity of each place. It was also, in his eyes, a form of 'diffused evangelism', leaving behind each time 'a group of Episcopalian Church people who, with their priest are encouraged and energised, able to relate to other Christians in the neighbourhood and with them, if possible, to witness and serve the total human conditions and needs of their communities.'

As always, he combined the capacity for severity bordering on the chilling with the utmost sensitivity and pastoral discretion with those who were in trouble with family or vocational problems. He could say to a potential ordinand, after an interview:

"I have an obscure and unshakeable conviction, no less obscure for being unshakeable, and no less unshakeable for being obscure, that *you ought not* to be ordained."

Yet several of his former clergy testify to the attention he paid to their own potential burn-out, or to the stress on clergy wives and families; and to how willing a listener he was to any request for support or advice in tricky situations. He believed strongly that the buck stopped with him when hard decisions had to be made, but appreciated the process of debate which preceded them, and had genuine respect for those who made a reasoned case for any position, even if it was not the one he himself took. And even years later, in his own retirement, he loved to keep in contact with those he had taught and had oversight of in his episcopate.

Two major developments which changed the shape of episcopal life in Scotland happened during his time of office. In the field of liturgy, the 1982 'Blue Book' was devised, tried and accepted. Its chief architects were three gifted members of the Liturgical Group whose skills Alastair admired and trusted: Bishop Michael Hare Duke, Gian Tellini and Brian Hardy, the latter two of whom had served on the staff of Coates Hall. Their combined talents of theological intelligence, sensitivity to language and appreciation of liturgical experience produced a text of extraordinary directness and freshness, without being remotely 'gimmicky'. On many occasions, both at home and abroad, Alastair quoted this 1982 Liturgy, loving its lack of churchiness, and its concentration on the cosmic and eschatological meaning of the gospel:-

"Through your Holy Spirit
you call us to new birth
in a creation restored by love."

"He is the Word existing beyond time
both source and final purpose
bringing to wholeness all that is made"

"That's what it's about", Alastair was wont to say. This liturgical emphasis was for him the bulwark against pietistic or church-centred readings of Christianity, a way of resisting "the terrible temptation, especially in a time of inflation, for the clergy to be 'bought', to become paid religious functionaries ministering to the felt needs of a congregation."

The other area of major reform was in terms of Church

government. Michael Hare Duke's essay in this volume testifies to the somewhat baronial understanding of Episcopacy which was enshrined in the Scottish Episcopal Church canons which had been inherited from the 19th century. It was Alastair's central concern that the Scottish Episcopal Church should be saved from any kind of nostalgic parochialism. Towards the end of the wrestling which changed the former Representative Church Council to a more open-textured General Synod, Alastair could preach crisply on the need for change.

> "This R.C.C. is dominated by two issues: first, the restructuring of our whole way of doing things: and second, our engagement in mission. Unless the first serves the second we waste our time. Futures may be unknown: options may be disputed; duties cannot be denied. What we are, as well as what we say, speaks either for God or against him. If new structures help us to be a better informed people, speaking more effectively in our society, our labour in creating them will be justified."

His preparation and thoroughness of detailed planning enabled him to carry the church with him, though there was much controversy along the way. There was enough of the statesman in him, in an almost Machiavellian sense of *realpolitik*, for him to confide in a friend,

> "If you've got to take a difficult decision in the Piskie church, take it in Inverness or Oban."

but he believed that all good decision-making had to be genuinely collaborative and made with a steady appreciation of the risks.

He also began the process which shifted the election of bishops from one weighted in favour of the local diocese to one which involved the collective wisdom of the church. This seemed to him a clear implication of what catholicity was about, a view endorsed by his predecessor and mentor, Francis Moncrieff.

Only occasionally he lost his public cool. He is on record as having been so exasperated in chairing one General Synod debate that he shouted from the edge of the podium "If you vote for this, you're a fool".

The effect was electric, and the vote went Alastair's way. But such explosive intervention was uncharacteristic. His normal mode was calm, measured and pragmatic, recognising the limits set in any given context by the politics and psychology involved in resolving conflict. Almost invariably, his concern was for what would maintain the catholicity of the faith, rather than creating sectarian ghettos of polarised opinion. But he never meant by 'catholicity' fluffy evasion of issues or pretending that there was agreement when there was manifest divergence. Candour about historical and contemporary fault-lines in the Christian tradition was for him vital to the commitment to truthfulness.

It was this which made him so valuable in the wider ecumenical contexts which he began to inhabit from the mid 70s. Within Scotland he had already had experience in the Anglican-Presbyterian Conversations of the 50s, which in the end became snarled up in Scotland over the question of episcopacy as vital to either the being or the well-being of the church. And at the local level he had a range of friends, contacts and visitors to his Dundee congregation and to Coates Hall who spanned the ecclesiastical divides. If they were lively, interesting, theologically stimulating people, they were welcome. His Episcopal consecration on 4th December 1975 was a widely ecumenical occasion.

He was not himself a rule-breaker. But he worked for and welcomed the relaxation of disciplines about eucharistic hospitality, and moved, albeit with some misgivings, to support the remarriage of divorced persons in church. In the area of church discipline, he followed William Temple on the character and virtue of Canon Law.

> "Strictly speaking a Canon is not a law at all. It is a rule expressing the general mind of the Church for the guidance of its offices and members... It is not in its essential nature something to be obeyed with mechanical uniformity until it is modified by the authority which promulgated it. It is to be obeyed with reverent regard, and followed with that freedom of spontaneity which belongs to the spiritual life for the regulation of which it is drawn up. Nothing could more conduce to the true welfare of our Church than a recovery of the original sense of canonical authority, as something which claims not detailed conformity, but reverent loyalty."
>
> (Preface to Ballard on the Standing Orders of the Church of England)

To some radicals, the distinction between reverent loyalty and detailed conformity might seem a distinction without a difference, but for Alastair it was a vital space for manoeuvre. And manoeuvres needed time. His primary malaise about radicalism, especially of the theological sort, was not really its content – (in some respects he was as radical as they come) – but its *pace*. For him, the long haul and the patience it required were truer perspectives on providential living than the urgent exclusivity of most radicals. He would sometimes tease his radical friends as "having no staying power".

From 1978 onwards, Alastair represented the Scottish Episcopal Church on the Board of the Division of Ecumenical Affairs, and within two years he had become its Chairman after Philip Morgan moved from that position to become General Secretary of the British Council of Churches.

All through the 80s he worked tirelessly on the widening circles of ecumenical life in the four nations, as the erstwhile largely white, largely long-established, largely traditional churches came to explore the implications of partnership with the more recently formed Black-led churches, and with Pentecostalist and Charismatic churches. The inclusion in the Board of representatives of such as Patrick Kalilombe from the Centre for Black and White Christian Partnership, Io Smith and Olu Abiola brought into the life of the Division an awareness that ecumenism could no longer be merely a pan-European matter, and reinforced the sense of global interconnectedness which has been an increasing part of Christian consciousness in the second half of the 20th century.

When the British Council of Churches initiated the 'Not Strangers But Pilgrims' process which was to lead to the Swanwick Declaration and the formation of the new ecumenical instruments in these islands, Alastair's role, both in public and behind the scenes, was vital, chairing the proceedings of the Steering Committee of the Inter-Church Process with his usual care and competence (no easy matter when over thirty denominations were attempting to negotiate structures in which all could conscientiously participate). It was also his personal character and abilities which helped to convince leading Catholics like Basil Hume and Derek Worlock that they had to be involved in the process, and that they could encourage full Catholic participation in the new structures.

One significant contribution to this was made by the Papal Visit to Britain in 1982 and the reciprocal visit to Rome by a group of B.C.C. and Catholic church representatives in 1983. In both contexts Alastair was aware of the significance of this encounter, and determined that the time should not be spent in mere formalities or courteous pleasantries.

During the Canterbury visit, Alastair was sitting next to the Pope on one occasion in Lambeth Palace, and began to describe the situation of inter-church families, one of the most existential concerns for the Division of Ecumenical Affairs. The pain of families separated at the Eucharist seemed to register, and few days later when the Pope spoke in York, and commended inter-church families as living in their marriage the hopes and difficulties of the path to Christian unity, that conversation was clearly in the background.

A year later, the subject was on the agenda again as part of a week of conversations with the various departments of the Curia, and in the audience with Pope John Paul, Alastair again pressed, courteously but firmly, for the urgency of addressing the issue. It was a personal disappointment to him that by the end of his life so little movement had actually happened towards changing the eucharistic possibilities for partners across the Roman/non-Roman divide, and that the Roman visit had made clear that the momentum of Vatican II reform was, at least in certain areas of Curial life, slackening visibly.

The spectrum was most palpably represented by, on the one hand, a visit to the Secretariat for non-Christians and, on the other, by an afternoon conversation with members of the Sacred Congregation for the Doctrine of the Faith, with Cardinal Ratzinger, its Prefect. In the former conversation, the majority of the staff, though mostly Catholic priests, had all been deeply exposed to life in non-Christian cultures, and were exploring the understanding of mission as a dialogue of mutuality between faiths, in which each learned truth from the other. In Cardinal Ratzinger's office, a question from John Habgood about the possibility of seeing the Magisterium as an approximation to the Truth provoked the response

"Unless God's truth is disclosed to us in absolute, determinate propositions, then salvation is at risk."

While Alastair had no doubts about the value of the visit as a rich encounter, not least for the depth of relationship it generated for the British delegation across their denominational diversity, he was clear from then on that significant process towards any kind of substantive unity would be a very slow business.

In spite of this, he retained his confidence that it was vital to that progress that, within Britain, the churches which had impressed the Pope by the quality of their ecumenical commitment should increase rather than diminish their practice of collaborative life. It was for the prize of creating a 'one-tier' membership, in which the Catholic churches of England, Ireland, Scotland and Wales could be full participant members that the old structures of the British Council of Churches were reshaped into the new Ecumenical Instruments of C.C.B.I., C.T.E., A.C.T.S. and C.Y.T.U.N. Chairing the Steering Group at the Inter-Church Process was, in a way, the culmination of decades of ecumenical involvement on Alastair's part.

Already back in the '50s he had been a member of the Anglican-Presbyterian Conversations, instituted by the 1953 General Assembly of the Church of Scotland. This was a quadrilateral dialogue, whose participants were the Church of England, the Church of Scotland, the Scottish Episcopal Church and the English Presbyterian Church. Alastair already recognised as a theologically literate and ecumenically open representative of the Scottish 'Piskies', was one of the younger participants, rubbing shoulders with giants like Donald and John Baillie, Archie Craig and Willie Manson.

It was an era of intense ecumenical endeavour. The establishment of the British Council of Churches and the World Council of Churches in the post-war years had fired many church people with a dream of re-uniting a fragmented church for witness and service. The 'Religion and Life' weeks of the wartime period had shown that for a large number of those outside the churches, denominations were an irrelevance if not a positive obstacle to participation in church life.

In Anglican-Presbyterian talks, the heart of the issue from a Church of Scotland perspective was certainly the question of Episcopal ordination, and whether it was necessary for either the being or the well-being of the Church. (As so often in ecumenical conversations, the 'ministry' issue is the one which seems to emerge as *the* neuralgic point.)

Alastair's participation was robust. With his Free Church upbringing, he knew from inside the concerns and anxieties of the Presbyterian soul, but found them, in the context of power in Scottish ecclesiastical life, somewhat surreal. One memorable exchange, which he himself recalled vividly some forty years later, ran as follows:-

Alastair: "This is ludicrous. The Church of Scotland being afraid of the Episcopal Church is like an elephant being afraid of a mouse, when it could swallow it up with one swoop of its trunk and not know that it had swallowed anything."

Archie Craig: "No, no, Alastair, you've got it all wrong. This elephant knows that the day it swallows that particular mouse, it will become an elephant that is fond of cheese and afraid of cats."

In a sense, Alastair embodied in his own person the particular charisma of the Anglican tradition: to be a kind of hinge between classic Catholic theology and ecclesiology and the virtues of the Reformation churches. But it is clear that his experience in the British Council of Churches during the '80s, in tandem with his widening knowledge of the global Anglican Communion, enlarged his sense of church. That, of course, was a microcosm of the global move from a complacently Eurocentric Christianity to recognition that the numerical shift of gravity to Africa and Asia had theological implications. The presence of representatives of black-led and Afro-Caribbean Churches in the B.C.C.; and in particular the establishment of Selly Oak's Centre for Black and White Christian Partnership under Bishop Patrick Kalilombe, were formative in the self-understanding of the Division of Ecumenical Affairs throughout the '80s.

For Alastair, the ecumenical imperative was not a matter of politeness, far less of prudent self-preservation. As he explicitly stated in a lecture to the Inter-Church Process, it was a sign of commitment and openness to the healing, providential purposes of God, an aspect of prayer more deeply than an aspect of politics:-

"Kneeling and listening in the presence of God with brothers and sisters in Christ from whom the accidents of history have divided us, and asking God how we may, together, learn the Gospel way of authentic reconciliation."

If however, prayer was the deepest level of his ecumenical commitment, it was not the only one. He had a shrewd and penetrating grasp of realpolitik and a confessed admiration for the skills of those who, in his judgement, like Basil Hume, could often circumvent confrontation by competent, unflamboyant anticipation of problems, diplomatic approaches to relevant personnel and a cool appraisal of risk.

Rarely one to go noisily public on controversial issues, Alastair's preferred strategies were more 'behind the scenes.' In the course of the life of the Inter-Church Process, he spent many hours of one-to-one conversation with leaders of different churches, interpreting the intentions and hopes and challenges of the evolving shift which led up to the Swanwick Declaration of 1987 and to the ratification by the churches of the new ecumenical instruments. He would have been the last to claim that he was more than the representative of either the Division of Ecumenical Affairs or the Steering Group of the Inter-Church Meeting. Certainly, he could not have advanced the process without the collaboration, energy, insight and experience of many trusted D.E.A. and B.C.C. colleagues; Philip Morgan, Colin Davey, Hugh Cross, Martin Reardon and many others. But these colleagues testify unanimously to his delicate role of advocacy, particularly in relation to full Roman Catholic participation in the new structures, which was so much part of the ground-breaking task.

Characteristically, he was also well aware of the pastoral dimensions of ecumenical change. Behind plans, shifting organisations, policy declarations, administrative and financial explorations were *people,* some of them in precarious and troubled employment situations, others less tangibly uneasy at such a major shift in the structures of ecclesiastical life in Britain and Ireland. Many of those involved, or in a position to be present at the heart of the process, witness to Alastair's unobtrusive attention to the personal aspects of the changeover, often through direct one-to-one contact.

In parallel with his deepening and demanding ecumenical agenda, the years as Primus of the Scottish Episcopal Church, from 1977 onwards, hugely extended his experience of the Anglican Communion.

While he had always been dutifully attentive to the overseas work of the church, and aware of global issues such as the race question in South Africa, he had not, for the first fifty-five years of his life encountered them first hand. He was dependent on reading of informed sources, and on contact with occasional visitors or trusted lectures. In Dundee, for instance, he made space for the congregation to hear the experience of Kathleen Dall, who had, as an S.C.M. worker, visited India. But on the whole, the brunt of his ministry there was to do with the understanding of faith as it affected the daily life and worship of the congregation, and the social and occasionally political life of the city.

Indeed, as a younger man, he expressed an active dislike of travelling, and confessed to having no desire to own or use a passport well into his fifties. It was one of his major conversion experiences to discover the excitement of travel, and from the mid-seventies onwards he put the Scottish Episcopal Church on the global map by his presence at all kinds of meetings, conferences and consultations.

Initially, most of these were to do with his structural representation of the Province, at Primates' Meetings for example: or with specific tasks delegated by the Archbishop of Canterbury, such as his visit to South Africa to investigate the treatment of Desmond Tutu by the apartheid regime. From 1979 onwards he was a member of the Anglican Consultative Council, and, with characteristic speed as his talents were recognised, became its vice-chairman from 1981 until 1985.

Friends who were in contact with him during these years testify, however, that he increasingly fulfilled such tasks not just with dutiful competence, but with zest. As his incisiveness, candour and salty wit were more and more widely appreciated, particularly in the North American context, he began to have invitations to travel in his own right, as preacher or lecturer; and his capacity for strong, convivial friendship flourished in this wider context. He was, invariably, the alert, questioning Alastair, reading up on the history and geography of wherever he went, and interrogating all comers about the local and national burning issues. But he also enjoyed the sheer variety of new experiences, exploring, in yellow oilskins, the tunnels behind Niagara Falls or trying out snowshoe walking in Newfoundland.

In the many anecdotes and reminiscences which were provoked by Alastair's death, and by the intimation of this tribute, there seems to be a significant watershed during his years as Principal of Coates Hall. Before then, the vast majority of summaries of memory contain words like 'austere', 'severe', and hint at a shade of authoritarianism which sometimes rubbed people the wrong way. Memories from those who met him from the '70s onwards are much more expressive of appreciation of warmth, geniality, humour and a kind of self-deprecating irony. The not uncommon phenomenon of age hardening people into rigidities of thought, feeling and practice was happily not Alastair's fate. He belonged to the other category who seem to mellow as time goes on, while never losing incisiveness or the willingness to champion his own convictions.

It was from his consecration as Bishop of Edinburgh in 1975 that the necessity of wider travel began to present itself, and by the time of his death in January 1998, he was reckoned to be the most widely-travelled Primus the Scottish Episcopal Church had ever produced. This might easily have generated some strain at the diocesan level (one of his colleagues estimated that there were times when he was physically 'off his patch' for as much as half of the calendar year.) However, two factors prevented that. One was Alastair's own organisational capacity and stamina, which meant that focussed preparation had always been made for his absences. The other was that he surrounded himself with a 'support staff' on which he had complete reliance, and to whom he could delegate responsibility with supreme confidence. His trust in his two secretaries, May Kingan and Christine Roy; in the clergy-team and vestry of St. Mary's Cathedral; and in the staff and officials of the General Synod Office gave him the freedom to go away knowing that the life of diocese and province were in capable hands. Indeed, Philip Crosfield, Cathedral Provost throughout Alastair's whole time as Bishop of Edinburgh, testifies to it as one of his gifts as a leader that, once he had identified the right person for a job, he would entrust them with huge levels of responsibility without constant scrutiny or interference.

A more intimate event also affected his capacity for travel. In 1979 his beloved wife Peggy died in the thirty-fourth year of their marriage. All through Alastair's strenuous ministries from Hendon onwards, she had been quietly supportive, both in terms of taking the lion's share in the care of their daughters, Alison and Mary Grace: but also in providing unobtrusive hospitality to the accelerating numbers who visited, especially

36

after the move from Dundee to Edinburgh. This was a costly sharing of ministry for someone who was temperamentally rather shy and self-effacing. In addition, much of her life was dogged by ill-health, including the side effects of medication.

None of this was compatible with globetrotting, and Peggy's gifts for gentle home-based welcoming of theology students, house guests and visitors from near and far was respected and appreciated by Alastair, who sought constantly to preserve the privacy of their domestic life as intact as possible.

In one of the obituaries written after Alastair's death, his friend and colleague Michael Hare Duke suggests that the deep sorrow at this bereavement was converted by Alastair into pastoral energy. It is also true that the standard risks for clergy spouses, of being torn between loyally to their partner's vocation and desire for more of their presence, would have been set to increase throughout the '80s, facing Alastair with complex and delicate choices. Instead, the energy travelled.

For a man one year off the standard secular retirement age, Alastair's stamina and multifaceted activities were impressive at local, national, U.K. and international levels. In his little neat diary, the pages were thick with meetings, conferences, lectures to be attended, pastoral visits, sermons to give. Yet he never appeared frenzied or driven. What he did seemed to be done with genuine relish, whether it was chairing residential weekends of the Division of Ecumenical Affairs, setting out on one of his pastoral visits to a parish in the diocese, or finding the space to attend a series of Gifford lectures.

During the '80s, there are possibly two overriding commitments which leave the Anglican Communion in his debt, in addition to his routine A.C.C. business.

One was the flurry of activity around the Bicentennial Celebrations of the consecration of Samuel Seabury to the Diocese of Connecticut. John Skinner, Bishop of Aberdeen, and Primus of the Scottish Episcopal church in 1784 had agreed to the consecration, an act of considerable risk and courage when his fellow bishops in Scotland were, on the whole timid about the risks of English resentment at the move. The relationship between Aberdeen and Connecticut was, in a way, the beginning of the American Province, the first step on the long road which was to make Anglicanism a world communion.

Alastair preached and lectured from New York to San Francisco and at multiple associated events in Connecticut itself, including one address to 15,000 people in the Hartford Civic Centre, where he undertook the challenge of trying to speak 'personally' to the largest gathering he had ever addressed. Typically, he had the detailed history of the Seabury event at his fingertips, politics, theology, consequences for Christian mission in North America. But, in fact, he spoke on his occasion about what for him was the core of the Gospel, namely the Philippians aspiration.

> 'That I may gain Christ and be found in him.... Not that I have already attained this, or am already perfect, but I press to make it my own, because Christ Jesus had made me his own.'

In a relatively rare autobiographical disclosure, he contrasted this aspiration, which was for him only realisable as part of the Body of Christ, the Church, with the more individualist appeal of his Free Church boyhood:

> "I was brought up in a Church in which personal commitment to Christ was looked for. One of my great

38

problems and distresses was that I could never identify with the experience of the people who bore witness to their understanding."

The Seabury event consolidated one of Alastair's strongest transatlantic friendships, with Arthur Walmsley, Bishop of Connecticut, a man who mirrors many of Alastair's own characteristics of intellectual integrity, generous ecumenical commitment, lively interest in literature and history, and gifts of hospitality and humour. It also gave him wide exposure on the North American scene, and led to many future invitations, and a deep sense of transatlantic links.

The second major ecclesiastical responsibility of the '80s which kept Alastair firmly on the international map was his appointment as Chaplain to the forthcoming 1988 Lambeth Conference. Since his appointment as Primus, and his involvement with A.C.C., Alastair's profile in world Anglicanism had grown hugely. The 1988 conference faced huge issues: questions which the whole church faced ecumenically about the relationship between classic tradition and contemporary culture; polarisation over gender/sexuality issues, particularly over gay and lesbian relationships and the ordination of women; debates about authority, concretely linked to the 1982 outcomes of the Anglican-Roman Catholic International Commission, (A.R.C.I.C.); and differences about the nature and integrity of Christian mission, especially in relation to other faiths. The 'broad church' tradition of Anglicanism, holding together a spectrum from 'low-church evangelical' to 'Anglo-Catholic' in an atmosphere of mutual, fairly tolerant co-existence was, it seemed, strained to breaking point by such tensions, and by pressures to specific, explicit alignments on doctrine, ministry and ethics from both right and left wing, many of them angry at what they perceived as a wishy-washy liberal fudge at the heart of the Anglican Communion.

It was, from the outset, a huge challenge for Alastair to plan what worship and pastoral care meant in such a context. Himself a proud defender of the liberal impetus in theology and churchmanship, he was plural enough in his history, experience and appreciation of the richness of Anglican tradition to contribute to a planning process which certainly made the 1988 Lambeth conference a re-affirmation of mutual commitment rather than a civil war. There was no smothering of debate, but the worship of the conference, and doubtless much behind-the-scenes pastoral interaction, kept making it convincing that once the commitment to belonging together was renounced, nothing creative could happen.

For me, as a participant, the microcosm of this was the bible study groups. As a Presbyterian, I might be expected to take to bible study like a duck to water; but in fact my experience of much formal 'Bible Study' is that it is timid, deferential, pietistic and deeply untruthful, in that most people feel cowed about bringing their real, human, emotional and intellectual energies to bear on Scripture. Latin America and Base Christian Communities have a bolder dynamic!

The Lambeth '88 bible studies, engaging with a brief, suggestive commentary by John V. Taylor on the Johannine 'farewell discourses', were an inspired event. For the whole three weeks of the conference, every weekday of work began with an hour's study of these few chapters of John's Gospel in groups of about sixteen, drawn from every context of race, theological background, pastoral experience and cultural assumption. The candour and indeed 'nakedness' of those committed encounters, building over three weeks into mutual trust and appreciation of sameness and difference were, for many, a worked example of Jacob 'wrestling with God', at a level of depth and intimacy which somehow modified the vast plenary discussions, and in some way affected their tone.

Characteristically, Alastair had been anticipating the scenarios of conflict, without any desire to mask them. But, characteristically too, he sought the least confrontational ways of addressing them. His choice of Assistant Chaplain, Mother Janet, OHP of Whitby, was no tokenism. The sisters of Whitby had been, for many years, part of the life of Scottish Churches House, Dunblane, the physical location of formal Scottish ecumenical activity for three decades. Mother Janet, as a full-time 'religious', was not ever going to be provocative as a bearer of the campaign for women's ordination. But Alastair knew, from his interactions at Dunblane and Whitby, that the luminous intelligence and openness of Mother Janet was bound to serve the conference. (She was, for instance, the first person to introduce to Dunblane Jim Cotter's paraphrase of the Lord's Prayer, with its bold opening:

'Eternal Spirit,
Life-Giver, Pain-Bearer, Love-Maker,
Source of all that is and that shall be,
Father and Mother of us all,
Loving God, in whom is heaven:'

Alastair's own advocacy of the ordination of women was, typically, a matter of 'resilient caution'. Some who knew him well felt that his head was perhaps ahead of his heart on the issue; but many of the testimonies after his death came from women who had found his active support well ahead of his time.

Rosemary Garrod, for instance, in the Newsletter of The Movement for Whole Ministry documents a meeting (undated) during Alastair's episcopate when she was the sole woman in a conference on stewardship. On the Sunday morning of the final Eucharist (Mothering Sunday) he asked her to take the chalice, and spent loving careful time exploring her resistance to the idea and consolidating his invitation. That episode triggered her eventual engagement with the Training for Ministry course.

What makes the Lambeth event even more remarkable is that it came, in the end, only weeks after Alastair had undergone major heart bypass surgery. No-one would have been surprised if, preparation done, he had called off. But from two days after his operation, he went into training; climbing stairs in the hospital to the permitted limit, and working out the bounds of his physical capacity. At the conference itself he paced himself judiciously, sometimes sitting when he would have stood; obviously cutting down on superfluous meetings and socialising: but a remarkably strong and capable presence in public, and as keen as ever in his fingering of pulses.

Again, it is Michael Hare Duke, friend and colleague who testifies, for instance, to Alastair's concern during the Buckingham Palace Garden Party on a hot 1988 August afternoon. While others socialised, Alastair buttonholed a surgeon rear-admiral who was responsible for medical provision at the event, and cross-questioned him, (doubtless with a shade of self-interest) about the details of coronary care provision for elderly prelates!

What is indisputable is that somehow, between the worship, the bible study, the pastoral attentiveness (totally private and undocumented) of the chaplains, and the general careful preparation of the whole event, the conference did not disintegrate, but committed itself anew to the painful exploration of what it means for the Anglican Communion to maintain solidarity in the face of huge named and recognised diversities and disagreements. The commitment to unity in a context of candour, acknowledged cultural difference, and the shared intention of loyal discipleship mirrored Alastair's own deepest sense of the church's calling.

Between Peggy's death and the 1988 Lambeth Conference, the most significant personal event for Alastair had taken place.

In 1983 he married Mary Scholes, former Chief Nursing Officer of Tayside Health Board and Chairman of the Scottish National Board for Nursing, Midwifery and Health Visiting. The years they had together until Alastair's death in January 1998 were a rich gift. Mary was able to share his hugely active 'retirement' with zest, and entered his many friendships in her own right. Travelling, particularly in the States, became a shared pleasure, and the lively comradeship manifestly suffused his restored health and wellbeing after the heart bypass surgery.

In his seventies and eighties, Alastair maintained a multi-faceted and energetic life. Within the family circle, he enjoyed, as always, his pride in Alison and Mary Grace, and from his engagement as grandfather he appreciated and learned about the pulse of the teenage world. Retirement allowed for the active cultivation of many friendships, some of them, as with James Robertson and Hugh McIntosh going back to his days as a theology student: others from later layers of his experience as teacher or pastor. His delight in catching up with former students or priests he had worked with, in following the news of their families and fortunes, was unfeigned.

On the church front, the Inter-Church Process continued to require major energy: and even when A.C.T.S. came into being in 1990, Alastair was deeply involved both in the Scottish Churches Agency for Racial Justice and its Agency for Inter-faith Relations. Lord Mackay of Clashfern, the then Lord Chancellor, remembers Alastair's insistent concern over the treatment of asylum-seekers; and his sense of the reality of a pluralist multifaith culture with which the church had to engage, was keen.

Invitations to preach both in the UK and overseas multiplied. Of the former, the near-legendary occasion was at the opening of the General Synod of the Church of England in Westminster Abbey in 1985, in the presence of Queen Elizabeth. Eye-witnesses testify to the smallest possible discernible pause as he turned a page. Then the sermon continued to its measured, lucid end. Only afterwards did it transpire that Alastair had turned the page to find the bulk of the sermon missing, inadvertently left in the vestry. Few vignettes offer better testimony to the psychological and intellectual 'cool' of a man on top of his material!

Of the overseas events, post-Seabury, one which Alastair and Mary both relished was an invitation to act as chaplain to a retirement community in Cape Cod, Florida. Many might have treated the visit as a pleasant sinecure. Alastair, as always, respecting the capacity of his community to respond to 'stretching', embarked on two courses of sermons which challenged his listeners to the full. Preaching, for Alastair, was never histrionic: but as he came to know the residents of this community, the low-key, calm, informative reflection on the character of honest faith in the contemporary world context built into an impressively consistent teaching ministry. Very different from 'one-off' occasional preaching, these sermons manifest a relaxed and happy interaction with a known congregation, where the deep seriousness of Advent and Lenten themes is offset by a wealth of shrewd anecdote, stimulating quotation and sometimes playful recognition of the context. The irony of preaching the Gospel in the comfort of Florida sunshine did not escape Alastair, but, characteristically, he set about the task with the firm conviction that those particular people in that particular context could be challenged to think just a bit better and more truthfully about their faith.

For his own recreation, as he notoriously entered in 'Who's Who', books, music and asking questions were the primary delights. The Edinburgh Book Festival was a high point in the calendar, and authors were pursued with stamina! Membership of the Society for the Study of Theology and the Society for the Study of Literature and Religion kept him in touch with current scholarship in fields which interested him, and his engagement, particularly with younger members of these bodies, was recognised after his death as a sign of generous encouragement and interest. The whole 'Gospel and Culture' project of Lesslie Newbigin, post 1984, fascinated him, though Alastair had little sympathy for the Enlightenment-bashing which was, it seemed to him, an increasingly dominant note within the movement. On a different scale, he enjoyed his regular commitment to meet at Roslin, where Roland Walls, Franciscan extraordinaire, hosted a small theological conversation of episcopal and theological density. His nickname for Alastair was 'l' Abbé philosophe', and the two enjoyed friendly sparring about what could and couldn't be thought and said!

In the '90s also, Alastair spent regular time as a volunteer helper with Threshold, an Edinburgh-based ecumenical network seeking to facilitate informal adult theological learning and dialogue. He would happily take his share in the chores of sticking stamps on envelopes for mailings, or help with the office rota, as well as making a signal contribution to the no-holds-barred discussions at monthly 'Open Forums'. On the evening of his final stroke he had in fact taken part, with characteristic vigour, in a discussion on how far congregations could be taken in the 'demythologising' of the Matthew/Luke Christmas stories. As usual, his contribution was like a small exocet missile!   To a speaker urging caution about disturbing people's confidence in the shepherds and the star, he recalled a Christmas Eve in Dundee when his young daughter had spontaneously asked, as she looked at the night sky: "Daddy, how exactly would you say what house a star was over?" The question delighted him, coming as it did, not from contrived theological sophistication, but from honest handling of experienced reality.

Theology apart, Alastair read voraciously, particularly in the fields of biography and history. He found the secular world fascinating, whether in the realm of natural science, or of political affairs. Peter Medawar was one of his heroes in the former sphere, not least because of his account of the role in science of being 'discovery-prone', alert and ready to identify the significance of data. And it was something of the same capacity for significant attention and 'reading' of facts which attracted him to journalists like Bernard Levin or Alastair Cooke. 'Letter from America' was a fixed point in his week, and his admiration for the marshalling of salient data, historical reminiscence and personal judgement into crisp, focused, economic prose was boundless. Even ecclesiastical processions sometimes had to wait till 'Letter from America' was over.

Fortunately, Alastair's final stroke did not impair him mentally. For that would have been, for him, the most painful of humiliations. He was an active defender of the principle of voluntary euthanasia, not because he wanted to make any general judgement about this or that quality of life being worthless, but because for him dignity implied the right to recognise it as a legitimate choice not to descend into the loss of selfhood which some human conditions entail. It was characteristic of his style that he never sought public controversy over the issue, but quietly pursued his commitments within the Society for Voluntary Euthanasia, clearly indicating the sense he had that absolutist positions about the 'sanctity of life' were an oversimplification. During the few weeks which followed the stroke he was well aware of his own physical impairment but able to sustain significant contact and conversation. He remarked wryly to one of his clergy that the physiotherapist was a little bit like God, both encouraging infinitesimally small signs of progress and then calling for further efforts! He even enjoyed a television programme about another of his human heroes, Isaiah Berlin, and retained his mental alertness throughout, as close friends shared what were to be his final weeks.

His funeral requiem was planned with meticulous detail to his own instructions: most significantly forbidding any eulogy, and vetoing any long painful procession of mourners greeting the family. In a packed St. Mary's Cathedral, representatives of every sector of Alastair's life shared a service of immense beauty and dignity, in which the interplay of light, music, classic solemnity and palpable human affection and esteem fused in the liturgical act. As Richard Holloway tenderly put it in his few preliminary remarks: "Lo, even from the grave, Alastair 'calleth the shots'!" He would have known they were good shots.

* * * * * * * * * * *

It would be impertinence to attempt to sum up so multifaceted a life and career. One of the remarkable things about it is that Alastair never attempted to publish his own sermons or essays. The Florida sermons were taped, mainly so that people could revisit them for further reflection; but, on the whole, sermons whose quality would be outstanding (by most reckonings) were scrupulously prepared for specific occasions and modestly filed away. In a sense, this reticence can be explained by Alastair's very genuine sense that he was not an original thinker. Several times he would make the public admission that

"I give you a posy of other men's flowers. All that is mine is the thread that binds them together."

That, however, seemed to him no failure, just as he though it no failure for a preacher, say at an evening service, to offer his people a sermon from one of the giants, Bonhoeffer or William Temple, being quite candid about its provenance. For him, the theological task, indeed the faith-building task was essentially collaborative, and he saw his own particular teaching/preaching vocation, in common with that of most pastors, as being a competent and accurate link between the tradition and the people. Though sometimes he spoke self-deprecatingly of his talent for 'haute vulgarisation', it was indeed a challenging and demanding vocation as he saw it, to help people reflect with integrity on the intersections between gospel and world.

By intellectual and political disposition he was classically liberal, though the label perhaps fails to catch the active tension he lived and felt between tradition and modernity. He quoted with approval an early formulation of Dick Holloway's about the 'permanent struggle between commitment to truth and equally necessary reverence before the tradition', and worked for an equipoise between the two which was dynamic rather than formulaic.

Newman, one of his theological heroes, was a frequent reference-point, particularly in his conviction that "Growth is the only evidence of life. To live is to change, and to be perfect is to have changed often." It was clear to Alastair that the world constantly gave rise to genuinely new knowledge – and the Darwinian, Freudian and Marxist revolutions in thought were paradigms for him, which the church ignored at its peril. He could be acerbic about intellectual sloth or what he regarded as the moral cowardice of evading such issues. Speaking to the Inter-Church Process in 1984, he remarked:

> "There are those who think that all we need to do today is to continue saying what our grandfathers said, only turning up the volume. It is not a view I share."

He relished and collected sardonic epigrams with which to sting those he regarded as; 'woollies' or 'soft-centred':

> "He threw some pseudo-light on non-problems" or "He deserves a V.C. for his cool intrepidity in the face of facts."

Such sentences were usually delivered, however, with a softening chuckle or an impish twinkle in the eye.

Though often accused of rationalism, Alastair's sense of the interplay between faith and reason was complex. He liked the Anselmian priority of faith seeking understanding, though he repeatedly made the eye-brow raising claim that, 'in a significant sense I have no faith of my own.' What he meant by that has to be interpreted by his sense of committed, ongoing engagement with all the big questions: about Providence, about the nature of the Christ-event, about what sacraments are, and about ethical and political decision-making.

Preaching in St. Mary's Cathedral on the Easter Sunday following the David Jenkins controversy about the Virgin Birth he began:

> "You might not believe it, but preaching at any time is a
> very hazardous engagement, not least on Easter Day:
> and for an Anglican bishop in the United Kingdom to
> occupy his Cathedral pulpit on Easter Day this year is
> an invitation to calamity."

Nevertheless, he believed that grasping bulls by the horns
was essential: and in the course of the next few minutes he
risked a tightrope-walk between robust refusal to say more
than he thought could be said and vital affirmation:-

> "The resurrection did not publicly vindicate anything.
> Jesus never appeared to those who did not believe in
> him."

But then, a few sentences later, lest anyone should think he
was settling for some private, subjective, pietist resurrection-
experience,

> "The inauguration of a new creation took place on
> Easter Day. Do I believe it? Yes, I think I do – as long
> as you don't try to push me into imagining that believing
> it means understanding it. I don't in the least."

The quest for theological truth was never, for Alastair, a purely
cerebral matter, though he deplored every attempt to underplay
the role of intelligence, or to sell it short. His fear of romantic
idealism or sentimental emotional spasms in religious life made
him capable of judgements like:

> "Even when our hearts are on fire, our brains must
> be on ice."

While well aware of his native and temperamental shyness

about physical contact among strangers, part of his growing appreciation of Anglican liturgy was that it accepted and sanctified all the senses, visual, tactile, olfactory, as well as the obvious hearing and tasting of word and sacrament. In many contexts he quoted with approval from what he regarded as C Lewis's best book, *'Till We Have Faces'*, where the princess of the old mystery religion affirms:

"Holy wisdom is not clear and thin like water, but thick and dark like blood."

So there was no question for him that the depth of faith was plumbed by the intellect: but no faith of integrity either which flew in the face of known or knowable facts. The historic commitment of Anglicanism to the interplay of scripture, tradition, reason and experience was, for Alastair, a working hermeneutic of great potency. The provisionality of theological discourse was for him a blessing rather than a problem, and he frequently commended the understanding of credal statement as a 'loose-fitting jacket', which was misunderstood if it became a straitjacket. "Theology is a 'hinty' language", he was wont to say to students and congregations alike: and his own appreciation of the 1982 'Blue Book' liturgy was that it was 'fey' enough to give space for such recognition of hints of transcendence.

One of his favourite and much-used prayers was from Bishop Ridding's Litany:-

"In times of doubts and questionings, when our belief is perplexed by new learning, new teaching, new thought, when our faith is strained by creeds, by doctrines, by mysteries beyond our understanding, give us the faithfulness of learners, and the courage of believers in thee: patience and insight to master difficulties,

51

stability to hold fast our tradition with enlightened interpretation, to admit all fresh knowledge of truth unknown to us, and in times of trouble really grasp the new knowledge and to combine it loyally and honestly with the old. Alike from stubborn rejection of new revelations and from hasty assurance that we are wiser than our fathers, save us and help us we humbly beseech Thee, O Lord."

As a nuanced aspiration, this lay pretty close to Alastair's heart, and it was his sense of balance in relation to its various components which kept him theologically and ecclesiastically located. On some issues, he was personally inclined to the radical end of the spectrum. He had almost no time for the idea of a second coming of Christ and a Last Judgement, and was outraged by the crypto-fundamentalism of much preaching on the topic. But he had strong realist convictions about the Holy Spirit.

"For the Christian, the words of Christ in the Gospel are not enough. They require to be supplemented and complemented by the guiding and teaching of the Holy Spirit today, in the hearts and minds of individual Christians, and in the corporate consciousness of the Church."

That process of discovering the 'corporate consciousness' was prospective as well as retrospective for Alastair: certainly not the re-iteration of a given deposit. It was what nerved his ecumenical commitment and his vigorous renunciation of De Quincey's judgement, "I am willing to follow Christ, as long as he does not come with his leprous bride, The Church."

For Alastair, such a perspective, shared by some radicals who sought a major polarisation between Christ and Church, was intolerable. He *expected* the tension between the shame and glory of the church to be perennial, part of the long haul of history, and sometimes teased his radical friends that they had no staying-power, no patience, no sense of time. As a matter of temperament, he admitted to pessimism: but the utterly fundamental sense he had of Christ's commitment to the church acted as a counterpoise, and he believed that the disciplined practice of the church's liturgical life was an indispensable implication of the Gospel.

On the aesthetic level, it was also for him, a deeply satisfying experience, and his care for the 'gravitas' and decorum of worship was constant, even occasionally an irritant to those who preferred more spontaneous or less structured forms of liturgy. Remarkably, however, the discovery of the multiple worship idioms of the members of the Division of Ecumenical Affairs or of the participants at the W.C.C. Vancouver Assembly made some impact. While he could never pretend to be happy or 'at home' singing jaunty choruses or listening to Pentecostal raptures, he had the grace to recognise that his habitual preferences were also limitations. So he could tease himself as well as others, announcing, for instance, in a Diocesan Newsletter, with mock-asperity. "Bill Brockie has cooked up some horrid, non-liturgical kind of brew to inaugurate this new relationship between St. Martin's and Wester Hailes."

It is difficult to catch in words the integrity of a character which had some of the qualities of shot-silk. To the recalcitrant student, or the ordination candidate who failed to convince Alastair of his vocational potential, there could be cutting negatives. Several recorded interactions testify to the severe pointing finger and the reiterated 'No, no, no, no, no!' Especially as a younger man, Alastair believed in leading from the front, and his sense of what it meant that the buck stopped with a leader remained unabashed. He had some self-consciousness about his public dignity, refusing to be seen eating fish and chips in the open air in Oban during a visit to plan the R.C.C. meeting: and protesting about a somewhat risqué postcard being sent by a curate from Paris, on the grounds that the postman would be scandalised! But both these episodes also reflect his natural fastidiousness and incapacity for squalor! Neatness and order were part of the grain of his being.

Cognate with that, he found it hard to cope with triviality: disdained Scrabble as a pastime; hated 'background music' which was not being properly attended to: deplored most hymns as unworthy: found scruffiness testing his patience: hated idling; could not begin to understand the impulse to 'loaf around'.

Such characteristics match the early adjectives: 'severe', 'austere', 'highbrow', but are only part of the story. For simultaneous and parallel accounts of warmth, geniality, affability and pastoral gentleness abound. Indeed, the two interpenetrated each other. For it was the cool, meticulous registering of dates, for instance, which meant that supportive pastoral contact could be made on significant anniversaries in the lives of parishioners, colleagues and friends. In an analogous way, it was the steady, painstaking, precise, cross-referenced annotation of books, periodicals and lectures which enabled sermons and addresses of an apparently painless range of reference, full of lively quotation and salient documentation of historical or sociological topicality.

To some these seemed somewhat chilly virtues, if virtues at all. But they were not, in fact, distant or abstract for Alastair, but part of his absorbed fascination with the detailed complexity of perception and exploration of truth. The quality of attention he expected and demanded from his ordination candidates in Coates Hall, his congregations in Kings Park and Dundee, his clergy colleagues as rector and bishop was, in the deepest sense, a tribute which he believed was an essential part of Christian Stewardship, a steady passion for truthfulness which could not be had on the cheap.

The overwhelming majority of tributes from those who contributed to this memoir were not focused on the austere rigorist with tendencies to severely authoritarian discipline of self and others. They reflect, rather, a man who learned to emerge from engrained Scottish reserve into a world of rich and convivial friendships: who had a gift for immediate rapport with small children and young people, becoming often a willing host in Edinburgh to the sons and daughters of friends: who was as interested in talking to the housekeeper in a friend's kitchen, or to local farmers on his visits to the Borders as to the 'great and the good'.

He had a wicked sense of humour: Elizabeth Salter, who was Moderator of the B.C.C.'s Division of International Affairs when Alastair was in Ecumenical Affairs recalls a visit in the late '80s to the Christian Peace Conference in Prague, where one particularly lengthy and ponderous patriarchal lecture of several hours duration had been endured. Straight-faced, Alastair made the summary comment:-

"I was very disappointed. He didn't once mention the Warnock Report."

His dry, ironic appreciation of human foibles, his own included, often released laughter in others. He loved, collected and shared aphorisms:

"Like all good slogans, it is something between a vague aspiration and a downright lie."

"The House of Lords is the only evidence for survival after death."

As a preacher, he was master of the arresting opening, often self-mocking.

"It is almost impossible to say anything on this subject without talking nonsense."

"I ask myself, as indeed you may ask yourselves, what on earth I am doing in this pulpit this morning."

"I am not sure what I felt like coming down to that music .... like something in a circus I think."

"I am absolutely appalled at being in this pulpit today."

On the whole, his humour was of the cool, tongue-in-cheek variety: "The Cathedral Chapter told me that nothing would give the Diocese more pleasure than that I should be away from it for four weeks." Such humour, combined with a vastly retentive memory for anecdote and a cosmopolitan range of interest, made him a lively conversationalist, whose table-talk was relished by many.

Alastair's own distaste for eulogy, far less for hagiography – *'De mortuis nil nisi bunkum'* – forbids such a memoir as this from concluding on any note of unqualified adulation.
Suffice to say that the range and depth of his friendships, the esteem even of those who crossed swords with him, or suspected they were politically outmanoeuvred, was truly catholic. The Episcopal Church in Scotland owes him, in large measure, a quiet, competent shift from relative provincialism and parochialism to a sense of participation in

church and world out of all proportion to its numerical strength. That, of course, goes hand in hand with the growing global consciousness of the Anglican Communion as a whole, in which Alastair was so willing a learner and so active a participant . His contribution to the new structures of ecumenical life in Great Britain and Ireland was immense, albeit unobtrusive. He had, by the end of his life, misgivings about whether the voiced intentions of the Swanwick Declaration were being followed through in spirit or practice, and was adamant that these new structures must be seen as provisional, and constantly subjected to candid scrutiny in the light of the Church's mission and witness.

His sense of destination, however, was firm. In the words of his beloved 1982 liturgy, what it was *about* was

"You call us to new birth in a creation restored by love."

Deeper than ecclesiastical realpolitik, deeper than penetrating intellectual enquiry, deeper than the ups and downs of human circumstance, that was his direction of travel, and his resilient hope.

Consecration Sermon

Thomas F Torrance

Sermon by T.F. Torrance at the consecration of Dr Alastair Haggart as Bishop of Edinburgh on Thursday, December 5th, 1975, in St. Mary's Cathedral, Edinburgh.

I should like to say how happy I am on this occasion both as a friend, a dear friend, of Alastair Haggart, and as a representative of the Church of Scotland, to participate in this service of consecration. This is an ecumenical act which signals a step in deeper unity in Scotland. Alastair Haggart's family and my own span both Episcopal and Presbyterian Communions. Our families are ecumenical units in themselves, and we rejoice in this act where that is sealed in the Consecration Service. We shall be welcoming your new Bishop as the Preacher at the Ecumenical Service to be held in Greyfriars Kirk during the General Assembly of the Church of Scotland.

In the Name of God, the Father, the Son, and the Holy Spirit, Amen.

Hear the word of God, from the l7th chapter of St. John's Gospel, verses 17-19, reading from the Revised Standard Version:

> *"Sanctify them in the truth. Thy word is truth. As Thou didst send me into the world, so have I sent them into the world, and for their sake I consecrate myself that they also may be consecrated in truth."*

Early in the 17th century, John Lightfoot, of Cambridge, the great Anglican Hebraic scholar, and the most learned of the Westminster Divines, who drew up the Westminster Confession of Faith, showed that some of the discourses in the Fourth Gospel are based on the Jewish Lectionary. Behind the 17th chapter of St. John, there lies, in part, the lectionary for Passover Week, which included Leviticus, chapters 7-9. That is the passage from the Torah, in which there are set out *the rites of the Consecration of Aaron as High Priest, and of the sons of his house.* Aaron only was anointed, but his sons were sprinkled with his anointing. Aaron only offered the sacrifice, but his sons had their hands filled with the oblations. And together they were vested as priests before the face of the Lord. The sons of Aaron were consecrated not directly but indirectly through the consecration of Aaron.

If that lies behind this prayer of Our Lord, it is not surprising that it has traditionally been called Our Lord's High Priestly Prayer - the prayer which He offered in his self-consecration as our only Mediator and High Priest, and which He fulfilled in His atoning sacrifice for mankind. In this prayer, Jesus tells us that He prayed first, not for the world, but for the disciples whom He had associated so closely with Himself, and whom He was about to take with Him into Gethsemane, and then for all who should believe on Him through them.

It is to this prayer of Our Lord's vicarious self-consecration that we turn now.

> *"For their sake I consecrate myself that they also may be consecrated in truth."*

In the ancient Ordinals, upon which Anglican and Episcopal practice is based, deacons are said to be made, presbyters ordained, and bishops consecrated. That distinction would seem to indicate that in the setting apart of the bishop, there is no additional or supplemental ordination, for, as St. Thomas Aquinas argued, *ordination is in order to the Eucharist*, and as such is complete. That is the ordination which is recapitulated and confirmed in the consecration of a bishop. Whatever else may be involved in this or that communion in the consecration of a Bishop, for example, by way of superior jurisdiction being conferred - and here the Churches differ - the main stress is laid upon *consecration* in which all ministry, in its appropriate way, partakes of the vicarious self-consecration of Christ. That is the aspect of the hallowing of the ministry distinctively stressed in the consecration of a Bishop, and that is *the innermost sanctum of the whole ministry - its relation to Christ.*

First of all, let us reflect upon that: *the relation of ministry to the vicarious ministry of Christ*, and today the relation of him, who is to be consecrated Bishop, to Jesus Christ. Jesus defines that ministry, in His prayer, by relation to Himself, thus, *"As Thou has sent Me into the world, so have I sent then into the world."* The ministry is rooted and grounded in the ministry of Christ Himself, in His own relation to the Father who sent Him. Jesus explains that relation in terms of his own vicarious self-consecration, for the ministry He sends is one that is implicated in His own self-consecration for them.

Today, immense emphasis is laid on the relation of the ministry to the world, and its involvement in the agenda that the world prescribes. But, here, when Jesus speaks of the relation between His servants and Himself, we see something rather different. The minister is not taken out of the world, but sent into it. Yet he is not of it, for he is consecrated and set apart by the most awful of consecrations, the Passion of Our Lord Himself. That is to say, in the world he is to exercise his ministry as *one who in his innermost life shares the consecrated life of Jesus Himself*, and that is the deepest significance of the consecration of a bishop. "Sanctify them in the truth, Thy word

61

is truth", Jesus prayed. On the inner hidden side of this life, there is a relation of oneness with Christ through sanctity and truth, which is fulfilled, as the Bishop gives himself to the Word of God and prayer. That is the inner discipline of the man of God, consecrated union with Christ in truth. But that is the most difficult aspect of the ministry. That arcane discipline, the hidden discipleship or soul struggle with the truth, and with commitment to Our Lord's self-consecration on their behalf. In this aspect of the ministry Jesus associates a man so closely with Himself that He takes him into the Garden of Gethsemane to watch and pray with Himself as He drinks the cup of sacrifice and sweats blood for mankind. "For their sake, I consecrate myself that they also may be consecrated in truth."

No man can engage in a true or proper ministry of the Gospel unless he constantly maintains this hidden link with Christ, and unless he cultivates this bond of sanctification and truth with the Lord. He has to wrestle with the Word of God - sometimes, like a flame of fire it scorches and burns him, for he must be purified, made transparent, utterly sincere, a trustworthy interpreter. He has to live so close to Christ that he even shares in the inner relation of Jesus to the Father, and partakes of His sanctity and truth. Only as such can he go forth into the world, be in the world, sent by Christ to minister the truth and the love of God, and tend the flock of Christ.

That is surely what consecration as Bishop must mean in the Lord: to be taken by Jesus Himself into the heart of His own self-consecration, to watch and pray with Him, even to be sprinkled with the blood of His sacrifice. No earthly support can avail for anyone in that awful experience where human flesh is utterly over-powered, but in the heart of it, Jesus prays for those whom He associates with Himself in this special way. He shares His own self-consecration as the great High Priest, with those whom He calls, and sets apart for holy ministry, and even when one of them fails and denies Him - as did Peter - Jesus still says, what He once said, "I have prayed for you, that your faith fail not." Therefore, let the new Bishop plant in the depths of his heart this awareness of Christ for him and in him: "I have prayed for you", and all the passion of Christ's self-consecration will avail to support and hallow his ministry.

Secondly, *there is implied here a contrast between true consecration, and consecration that is not ultimately real*. "For their sake, I consecrate myself that they may be consecrated in truth", or as we may indeed translate the Greek "in reality". The focus of attention is on the vicarious self-consecration of Christ. That is the real thing. It is not the ceremony as such that counts - all that one reads in the book of Leviticus, or indeed all that one may read in an ancient or modern ordinal - but what actually takes place in Jesus Christ, the stark and utter simplicity of the truth as it is in Jesus.

That is, I believe, the way of unity: the kind of unity with which Our Lord is concerned from end to end in this high priestly prayer. For a number of years, I worked on a special Commission of Faith and Order on the relation of the one Baptism to the one Lordship of Christ. That was presided over by a Lutheran Bishop as its Chairman. It had as its secretaries, an Anglican, and a Baptist, together with an Orthodox (Georges Florovsky), a Quaker, Reformed, Congregational, other Anglicans, and Lutherans - about fifteen in all - who participated, over a period of five or six years. The more we concentrated on the objective reality of Baptism in Christ, the greater the agreement, until total agreement within the group was reached, which was, to me, a deep lesson in unity. And now the Faith and Order Commission of the World Council of Churches is attempting to do the same in regard to the ministry and the Eucharist, with considerable success. The Churches of Christendom differ over the ministry more than anywhere else, but if we focus upon the real thing - the vicarious self-consecration of Christ to ministry - then we do find real unity cutting behind our differences, and the differences begin to become superficial and fade before the reality. And that, I believe, to be the real intention here today. The planned simplification of the ceremonial, especially in respect of the installation, a Presbyterian preaching the sermon, the participation of all in the Eucharist, are highly significant. The focus of attention is directed beyond, across our ecclesial differences upon the one Christ, the only Mediator, the one High Priest, the only Bishop and Lord of our souls - to the unique self-consecration of Christ on our behalf. As we do that we learn that our Lord prays not only for his apostles or bishops or ministers, but for *all* who are to believe on Him through their word that they may all be consecrated together in one, even as He and the Father are one. "I in them and Thou in me that they may be consecrated in one so that the world may know that Thou hast sent me, and hast loved them as Thou hast loved me."

And, finally: *our Lord's high priestly prayer of self-consecration on behalf of his servants was offered in connection with the Holy Supper*, which He celebrated with His disciples, "For their sake I consecrate myself that they also may be consecrated in truth". It is not surprising, therefore, that from earliest times ordinations and consecrations took place in an eucharistic context. Or to put it the other way round, the celebration of the Eucharist occupied an essential place in the consecration of a bishop, as it does here today, for it is properly and ultimately through eucharistic communion in this context that he shares in the vicarious self-consecration of Christ.

In the Old Testament rite, described in Leviticus, the consecration of priesthood was brought to its completion in the "filling of the hands" of the priest with the oblations, and in the sacrificial meal of flesh and bread called "the sacrifice of praise and thanksgiving". And so in the Apostolic Constitutions of the 4th/5th century, we learn that consecration - or ordination as the case might be - is brought to its completion when the person consecrated, takes the bread and wine into his hands, and celebrates the Eucharist. *The real celebrant at every Eucharist is Christ Himself*, for the only real offering is Christ's Self-offering - that offering which he made on our behalf when he took our nature upon himself, and when He offered Himself through the eternal Spirit without blemish to the Father. The fact that He ever lives before the Father, presenting Himself and us in Himself before the Father, is the ultimate reality behind our eucharistic celebration on earth. Is that not how we are to understand what takes place today? When the bishop being consecrated is associated with the Primus as president of the Eucharist, and the other bishops, in celebration of the Lord's Supper, it is Christ alone who is High Priest. He alone is the one mediator between God and man who offers Himself on behalf of these His servants, and on behalf of the new bishop that he may be consecrated together with them in and through Christ's self-consecration.

There is an old oblatory formula which we can trace back at least to the young Athanasius in the early 4th century, and is to be found in the old *Ordo Romanus* in the 6th century, which our Roman brethren still use. "Through Him, and with Him, and in Him, is to Thee, God the Father Almighty, in the unity of the Holy Spirit, all honour and glory" - not only through Him, and in Him, but "with Him". It is none other than Jesus himself who prays and is present, and does that for our sake, and on our behalf, *with us*. He invites us to pray and worship the Father through Him, and in Him and with Him.

Thus, in the last analysis, it is the Lord Jesus Himself who puts the bread and the wine into the celebrant's hands, and bids him celebrate the Eucharist, and dispense the bread and wine as the body and blood of Christ in consecrated union with Himself. This is a consecration in which we are all invited to share as we partake of the body and blood of the Saviour, each in his own personal self, each in his own distinctive place, or office, in the membership of the one body - all in such a way that as each is made to share in the one vicarious self-consecration and self-offering of Christ, we are consecrated together into a unity in the Lord.

Let that be our prayer, brethren, as we from different churches join here with the Scottish Episcopal Church in the consecration of Alastair Haggart to be Bishop in Edinburgh, recognising that he is consecrated not only as Bishop of the Scottish Episcopal diocese of Edinburgh, but as servant of the Lord in the one Holy Catholic Church, which embraces us all, recognising that he is consecrated in the Lord in such a way that it is the Lord Jesus alone whom we serve and worship as King and Head of the Church; but let it be our prayer that, as we join together in eucharistic celebration through, with, and in Jesus Christ our only Mediator and High Priest, we may indeed be consecrated together into that profound unity which is a sharing here and now, of the unity of the Father, and the Son, and the Holy Spirit.

Now, a prayer from John Calvin:

"Almighty God, as thou has been pleased in thine infinite mercy not only to choose from among us some to be priests unto Thee but also to consecrate us all to Thyself in Thine Only Begotten Son, grant that this day we may purely and sincerely serve Thee and so strive to devote ourselves wholly to Thee, that we may be pure and chaste, in mind, soul and body, and that Thy glory may so shine forth in all that we do, that Thy worship among us may be holy and pure and approved by Thee, until we

shall at length enjoy that glory to which Thou dost invite us by Thy Gospel, and which has been obtained for us by the blood of Thine only begotten Son."

And now through Him, with Him, and in Him be to Thee God the Father Almighty, in the unity of the Holy Spirit, all honour and glory. Amen.

Footnote
[1]Sermon preached at St. Mary's Cathedral, Edinburgh
Reprinted from *Ekklesiastikos Pharos, III-IV, Athens, 1976, pp.226-231*

Human Uniqueness

John Habgood[1]

I shall not waste much time trying to prove that human beings are unique within the animal world. It seems to me self-evident. Though there are other highly social animals, there is nothing else remotely equivalent to human culture. Moreover, the fact that the context of this lecture is a discussion of our own evolution, is proof of one of our unique attributes – our capacity for self-reflection.

I am not, of course, claiming that human beings are unique in every respect, because plainly we are not. We have evolved like other animals, and we share with them a great deal physically, mentally and socially. Many individual human attributes can be found, at least in embryo, in one or other species. Nor does it make any difference, in my view, whether we evolved entirely through a process of natural selection, or whether selection was supplemented by some other means. Natural selection is not alien to our human world. We can see it at work in the rise and fall of nations; we can see it in our frustrated attempts to beat the evolution of bacterial resistance to our medicines; and we can see it in just about everything around us, as ideas, techniques, goods, services and so on, are constantly discarded to be replaced by more effective ones. Our uniqueness lies, neither in our origins, nor in the processes of our development, but in what we have come to be.

For instance, the fact that we can make good guesses about how language might have evolved from much more primitive forms of communications, does not detract from its present power to shape and sustain our processes of thought far beyond that of any other living thing and beyond the immediacy of physical experience. Imagination, I suspect, is uniquely human. We are also unique in our uses of symbol and metaphor.

Or again we can see how the necessities of social life, and the lengthy process of nurture, may well have provided the impetus for the development of altruism. But this is only the first step towards ethical obligation, a concept unique to human beings in that it involves, among other things, conscious reference to general principles.

Similarly, theories about the origins of religion in the fear of death, or the need for tribal unity, or in the sense of awe at natural wonders, do not invalidate the recognition of, and respect for, the sacred. In fact the great world religions have become enormously fruitful and highly sophisticated explorations of aspects of experience, which from the start have been central to human life. To explain something away in terms of its origins is to ignore one of the main lessons evolution can teach us, namely that new qualities and capacities can emerge from apparently unpromising beginnings.

So much by way of preamble. When we turn to the different ways in which human beings have thought about their own nature, and how these have been articulated in religions and philosophies, the picture is much less clear. One could describe it in very general terms by saying that there has been an almost universal reluctance to identify human beings solely with their physical forms. Persons are different from things. We shrink from treating ourselves, or other people, as mere objects. This is not to deny the immense importance of the physical basis of personality, all the more so as its complex structures are unravelled, and our powers to change it by physical or chemical means are frighteningly increased. But even so there are few who would want to deny special status to living persons as subjects in their own right, subjects with whom we can communicate and share a sense of inwardness, and who are thus worthy of respect and care.

How is one to express this special status? The language of 'having a soul', or 'being a soul', has been the most common description among Christians, Jews and Moslems, as well as in classical philosophy. Most other religions, though they use different words, have broadly similar concepts – Atman in Hinduism, for instance. Without going into details, one could say that the perception that we are more than our bodies has until recent times been near universal.

In the Platonic tradition the soul was envisaged as a kind of non-material entity, an eternal and pre-existent something inhabiting the body, and capable of existing without it. It was a notion which had powerful influence on early Christianity, and there are even traces of it in parts of the Bible, particularly in the Wisdom literature. "The souls of the righteous are in the hands of God, and there shall be no torment touch them." (Wisdom 3, 1) We find this same notion of the soul as an independent entity in faiths which teach the idea of reincarnation. There are even claims to some sort of empirical verification in stories of memories being carried from one life to another. And, increasingly nowadays, there are numerous stories of near-death experiences in which the centre of consciousness seems to have become detached from its body, and hence able to observe what is going on from a different viewpoint. But there are also absurdities, as when in the late 19th century the entity theory of the soul was supposedly tested in experiments to detect its departure by weighing people on an ultra-sensitive balance at the time of death.

The modern form of body/soul dualism owes its origin to Decartes. For him the absolute distinction between body and mind or soul was the rational basis of all certainty. The one thing we infallibly know is that we ourselves think, and if this makes the material world seem problematic, then so be it. Mind or soul is primary, and the reality of the world as perceived can be guaranteed by the belief that God does not mislead us. This is the exact opposite of modern materialism, which has no use for the soul, and questions whether the self exists at all, or whether it is merely a social construct. Indeed the history of Western philosophy in the last four centuries is the story of the difficulties to which Cartesian dualism gave rise, not least the problem of how a non-material mind or soul could have evolved, and how it could possibly interact with its body.

More hopeful is the alternative approach, originally set out by Aristotle, and in due course incorporated into classical mediaeval theology, as represented by St. Thomas Aquinas. According to Aristotle the soul was not a separate entity at all, but was the 'form of the body'. Form is what makes a thing what it is. It is what makes this lump of flesh a human being. More precisely, the soul was seen as the animating principle of the body, what makes living things alive, a concept which in recent years has returned to favour among many Christians in view of its parallel with some Old Testament ideas. Hebrew thought was similarly non-dualistic. A person is a psychosomatic unity animated by the breath of life from God.

The difficulty with this idea, of course, is that the concept of an animated body smacks too much of vitalism to be readily acceptable to those familiar with modern biology. But Aristotle and his successors were more subtle than that objection might imply. There is at least a partial analogy to what Aristotle meant by 'form' in our present notion of 'organised complexity.' Organisation is not an extra ingredient added to a mixture of non-living materials. It is the form in which they must exist if they are to be alive. There is a rather different analogy in the relationship between a word and its meaning. The meaning of a word is not something added to it, as one might add an extra letter of syllable. It is the word perceived, not merely as a collection of letters or sounds, but as the significant element within the process of communication between persons.

In effect, what I am suggesting is that we can view the same reality from different perspectives. To know a person's mind, or to discern their soul, we have to relate to them. There are things we can learn through the objective study of what is physically present, whether bodies or movements or sounds or smells. But there is another level of understanding which is only possible because we belong to the same human community and can share meanings and feelings and a common experience of being alive as persons. In a sense this is so obvious that it is easy to overlook it, but it is the fundamental reason why we rightly regard human beings as unique.

We are what we are as persons because a unique potential has been developed in each of us through the relationship within which we stand. To that extent the self *is* a social construct. But from a religious perspective the fundamental relationship which encompasses all others is our relationship with God. It is this relationship, Christians claim, which endures when death dissolves earthly relationships. Or as I have put it myself in a different context, our unique and enduring identity is what we are in the mind of God.

Understanding human beings in these relational terms can throw some light on the significance of human development and decay. There does not have to be a sharp dividing line between the pre-human and the human in the process of evolution. It is enough to postulate a gradually developing self-awareness through the growth of language, social interaction, and relationships with 'significant others'. If it is true that religion was the matrix within which culture was formed, then the most 'significant other' was transcendent. One can thus begin to see how human self-awareness and awareness of God might have formed and shaped one another. It is in this sense that we can describe ourselves as made in the image of God.

I offer this as an alternative description of what is meant by the soul. It has obvious implications also for the way we think about the development of individual human persons. The belief held by some Christians that a soul is implanted in an embryo at the moment of conception seems to me highly implausible, quite apart from all the difficulties I have mentioned in treating the soul as some kind of pre-existent entity. But the idea that a personal relationship begins to be formed fairly early in the womb, and that a new individual grows in personhood as this relationship with other human beings is filled out after birth, seems to me to make good sense of actual experience. The belief that these human relationships are to be understood within an overarching relationship with God, mediated through other persons but also transcending them, gives them at every stage a greater significance. It is this transcendent relationship which then forms the basis for the respect due to human embryos, as known to God before they are even known to their parents.

Decay and death at the other end of life can be seen as following a similar pattern in reverse. The gradual loss of earthly capacities should not be seen as diminishing the unique value of people who are reaching the stage when they are beyond human contact, and are known in their fullness only to God. I have described this process elsewhere as the "handing back to God of what has been lent us." It is consistent with the long-held Christian belief that a kind of stripping down is necessary as we approach the time when our whole being is sustained by God alone. This awareness of a larger context in which decay and death are to be understood has implications for medical practice. To allow people to die with dignity and, when appropriate, to know that they are dying, is part of the respect we owe them as unique individuals. But we also have to be aware that part of that uniqueness is embodied in a unique set of relationships which also have to be respected, and that is why deception at the onset of death can sadly diminish people.

Darwinian medicine may also remind us that death is a necessity if there is to be more life. And that is an insight Christians can also share, albeit with some rather special connotations.

Footnote
[1]Lecture originally delivered to the Royal Society of Medicine. Conference on Darwinism, 15th February, 2000. Internal references to *Being a Person: Where Faith and Science Meet.* John Habgood, Hodder and Stoughton 1998

Formation and Freedom

John Clarke

Students who trained at Coates Hall in the early 1970's knew Alastair Haggart as a powerful role model. Some struggled with him, suspecting him of over-intellectualisation and arrogance. Others found his combination of self-discipline and breadth of vision a refreshing antidote to sentimental piety. Few could have doubted that he cared passionately both about theology and about the formation of ordinands.

Twenty-five years later I have had the privilege of leading another theological college, Ripon College, Cuddesdon, and have found that Alastair's way of being a priest continues to challenge and inspire me.

The context of ministry has changed. We live now in an age where theology increasingly finds itself at the margins of intellectual debate and in which there are increasing discontinuities in the transmission of faith. We cannot assume a knowledge of the Bible and Christian tradition amongst churchgoers let alone amongst the wider population for whom Christianity has become one choice within the supermarket of faiths. But, in spite of the decline in churchgoing, the search for enduring truth continues, and in this demanding pursuit Alastair showed an openness and honesty that can still renew and humble.

I want to focus on three aspects of the model that Alastair offered to his students and to his clergy. The first is that the ordained minister is a man or woman who is claimed by tradition and lives to rework and reinterpret that tradition. The second is that the ordained minister is called to offer the world to God in all its variety, and must not seek escape in a religious sub-culture. The third is that the ordained minister may need to deconstruct the visible forms of church life to allow the eschatological space in which God may be found.

Ordained ministry and the discipline of tradition

The Jewish philosopher, Emmanuel Levinas, has written a Talmudic commentary in which he reflects on the paradox that the people of Israel commit themselves to do the Torah before hearing it. The title of the commentary, 'The Temptation of Temptation[1]', contrasts this religious subjectivity willing to submit freedom to an as yet unknown tradition, with the desire of Western culture to know all things, experience all things and yet remain free and unaffected by all temptation.

The Jewish emphasis is upon praxis, upon obedience to the ritual and ethical commands of the Torah. Reflection upon the meaning and interpretation of the action comes afterwards, and is forever subordinate to the performance of the deed.

Tradition carries different overtones in Christian theology. Disputes about doctrine can make it seem a question of right belief rather than right action. But doctrine is not formulated in a vacuum, it comes out of the ecclesial life of worshipping communities. As the WCC study 'Confessing the One Faith' puts it

"The apostolic faith is expressed in confession, in preaching, in worship and in the sacraments of the Church as well as in the credal statements, decision of councils and confessional texts and in the life of the Church. Theological reflection has always rendered a service to the confessing community by seeking to clarify the faith".[2]

Theological reflection is inevitably plural, drawing upon the cultural and intellectual inheritance of both writer and audience. Ecclesial traditions are also plural, and can tend to be exclusive and competitive. But tradition can be uniting, if it is not conceived solely in doctrinal or institutional forms, but is recast in eschatological terms as a movement in the Holy Spirit towards the end of reconciled diversity that has been foreshadowed in creation. For, already, through the gift of speech, human beings have been opened to listen and give to each other. Tradition unites only if it is recognised as the history and future of God's presence enacted in the generosity of his people.

Every Christian, and above all those called to the ordained ministry, needs to be rooted in this tradition of the indwelling of God. This rooting is first of all about belonging and doing. It is about the discovery of a new identity grounded in the free gift of grace within a worshipping community. This identity does not abstract from denomination or from culture but opens these to a network of relationships that are not founded on exclusion. The determining identity of the person comes not by self-definition, but from God and is embodied in action. It reflects the words given to Jesus in St. John's Gospel "You did not choose me, but I chose you and appointed you that you should go and bear fruit and that your fruit should abide" (Jn. 15 v 16)

This naming and calling by God, runs counter to a belief in the primacy of conceptual knowledge, and makes obedience to the purpose of God a prerequisite to faithful living. And yet on many central issues, such as the ordination of women, the acceptance of gay people or the response to people of other faiths, deep divisions exist within the church. Conflicts of interpretation and culture are all too obvious. The unity of the church through space and time can only express being in

Christ as it seeks to listen to contradictory and neglected voices and to challenge those whose identity has become fixed. It is only a people faithful in its longing for the end that is its future in God, that can face up to passionate argument and still offer a theology that is both truthful and concerned to heal.

In practical terms this means that entry into faith and growth in faith involve both a surrender of will, and openness to the leading of God. Christians require humility to learn from those whose practice of faith is more established and settled. Most students who enter training at a theological college have been inspired by the patterns of discipleship of particular people, to offer themselves for ministry. In their study they encounter theologians and church leaders whose words and practice expand their understanding of God and their vision of the church. In the rhythm of daily worship they realise a communion that goes beyond the visible church and unites them with the saints who have grown into the fullness of Christ.

Alastair knew the line of continuity embodied in the lives of the faithful. His disciplined belonging was a recognition that he continued to be a learner from the faith of others. It was the acknowledgement of a proud and sometimes stubborn man that he was responsible before God for the considerable personal and institutional power that he exercised. It was based on a day by day trust and expectation that God wanted to reshape and reform his people.

Ordained ministry and the offering of the world
From within a settled practice of faith can grow a critical engagement with the contemporary world. The world of prayer and liturgy is too often an insulation from the flux of contemporary life, trapping the worshipper in archaism or

using words and music whose cultural challenge has been blunted by familiarity. It can, though, be a basis from which to move out. Alastair's radical edge combined the desire to question and reformulate the content of belief with an alertness to the costs of social exclusion, and a willingness to grapple with new ethical issues thrown up by advances in medical knowledge.

But this process cannot be only one way. There comes a time for liturgical revision, when the key texts of a denomination are reworked in the light of new theological understanding, or the changing reference of language. Prior to this there may be a multiplicity of attempts to try out new metaphors and forms of prayer appropriate for particular contexts. All age worship, urban deprivation, new forms of community life, feminist imagery of God, or ecumenical events may provide the stimulus for creative experiment which is then tested by the church before entering the mainstream of liturgical practice. Although the process of reception is inevitably cautious, this should not depress the liturgical innovator.

Conversely, a certain stability of form can enable a deeper entry into the poetry and mystery of worship, and an acceptance of the given allows energy to be directed beyond the church in engagement with currents of intellectual and social change.

The possibilities for liturgical variety in the Anglican Church have increased rapidly in the past twenty-five years. Amongst students preparing for ordination now there are some who regret the passing of the kind of uniformity represented by the Book of Common Prayer, and there are others who find any normative order a straitjacket which restricts spontaneity and creativity.

In the practice of Ripon College Cuddesdon we try to hold together a consistent rhythm of prayer within the Daily Offices and Eucharist, with regular opportunities for greater flexibility. A Taizé based service, worship using material from the church in Sri Lanka, a meditation using the poems of R.S.Thomas or the music of John Tavener can complement the more prosaic style of the Alternative Service Book, or Common Worship.

But the deeper question of the link between church and kingdom remains vital. There is a conservatism concerned with the flourishing of the institutional church of whatever form, that avoids questions of truth or social justice. It is exciting, though unfortunately relatively rare, to find ordinands committed to the transformation of the political and economic order, or who are grappling with the meaning of the new world of genetic engineering, or who are alert to the necessary interplay of faith and doubt in fashioning appropriate language in which to speak of God.

Placement experiences in churches, hospitals, schools, prisons, and other social agencies have become an established part of ministerial training. Pastoral reflection and courses in mission and ministry have attempted to make the link between church and community more explicit. In spite of this there are still many whose first concern is about the role of the clergy rather than the wider activity of God in the secular.

It was one of the strengths of Alastair's ministry that it was rooted in the world before his detailed concern for the church. The security of his practice of faith gave him a freedom to explore contemporary issues and to see how they related to the preacher's task of articulating the hope that is within us.

This is a way of thinking at one with John Robinson's description of the church as the instrument of the kingdom. It is alert to the ecclesiastical trap that Robinson described when he wrote that "the perennial temptation of the church is to equate itself with the kingdom of God on earth, and so regard itself as the agent of God in this world."[3] In this engagement the task of theology is less to defend credal or doctrinal orthodoxy than to inform and criticise moral choices and the experience of everyday life.

The sermons of Desmond Tutu in the apartheid era offered a vision of barriers of race being broken down, and the emergence of a 'rainbow people of God'.[4] Thomas Merton used the language of monasticism to reflect about peace-making and the spiritual insight of other faiths.[5] Rowan Williams has recently written a book, 'Lost Icons'[6], in which he draws attention to the loss of childhood and the language of remorse in our culture. Theology here exists for an audience outside the walls of the church building.

In such writing the engagement of theology with the boundaries of knowledge of other disciplines becomes critical. The learning has to be two way. Just as theology can help the wider community to become more aware of certain features of the moral landscape, such as the possibility of sanctity or the persistence of evil, so advances in astronomy or the mapping of the human genome must be allowed to modify Christian language about the place of human beings in the universe.

But the dialogue runs deeper still, for on many occasions it is an internal conversation that exists in different forms within church and society. Although it appears that internal issues such as sexuality, lay presidency, the ordination of women and the interpretation of the bible dominate the agenda of the churches, these need to be seen in the wider context of society's questions about human identity, hierarchy and tradition. Theology can help them to take their place in speech about the kingdom, in God's desire for the reconciliation of all things in Christ.

The terms of ecclesiastical debate may be couched in the strange and increasingly narrow world of religious language, but they are not so far from the concerns of most people. Within the life of a parish the ordained minister can use the role of preacher and teacher to open up contemporary questions to discussion and debate. This may involve listening to voices of expertise and wisdom from outside the church. It will certainly require the ability to put theology to work and to make connections that bring both freedom and insight. There is a variety of models here to adapt and follow, ranging from the experience of base communities in Latin America, or the parish meetings of Alan Ecclestone in Sheffield in the 1950's, to the welcome that some cathedrals have offered to intellectual debate and to the contemporary visual and dramatic arts.

The Orthodox theologian John Zizioulas writes that "The ministry relates the church to the world in an existential way, so that any separation between the Church and the world in the form of a *dichotomy* becomes impossible. As it is revealed in the eucharistic nature of the church, the world is *assumed* by the community and referred back to the creator. In a eucharistic approach it is by being *assumed* that the world is judged, and not otherwise."[7]

This is a theological and liturgical vision that goes further than verbally linking church and world by preaching and teaching. It suggests that the Eucharist is an event that embraces the world and seeks to build relationship to all that is still separate from God and unfulfilled. Indeed it is communion, and its acceptance or refusal that brings judgement on people and nations. The power of this intimate offering of the world to God by the church is rarely glimpsed. Perhaps the sharpest examples in recent history are provided by the fusion of liturgical and political action in the Solidarity movement in Poland, and the challenge of multi-racial worship in apartheid South Africa. Here we can see that the sacrament of the Eucharist points to a transformation that is beyond thought and ideas and involves the renewal of bodies, of social and economic structures, as well as spirit.

But there remains a task of recovering and renewing the meaning of liturgical symbols so that they move beyond the realm of the religious cult and become bearers of meaning for the wider society. How can we celebrate the material of water, bread, wine and oil, and show that they connect to the world of the internet, the high rise flat, and the language and culture of young people?

In part this will depend on particular moments of tragedy and triumph, when the latent religiosity of a culture finds expression through the Christian story, which reveals the world as both flawed and good, and which enacts God's yearning for its completion. But preparing for and shaping these times of transfiguration requires the interpretative skill of the ordained minister who is alert to the need of the church for the world and of the world for the church. The focus of this interplay is the life and passion of Jesus, for, on the cross, all separation of the religious and the secular is brought to an end. As it says in the report 'Baptism, Eucharist and Ministry', 'In order to fulfil its mission, the Church needs persons who are publicly and continually responsible for pointing to its fundamental dependence on Jesus Christ, and thereby provide, within a multiplicity of gifts, a focus of its unity'.[8]

Ordained ministry and the deconstruction of the Church
It is suspicion of false claims to totality that makes the institutional church problematic. All denominations have a remarkable ability to claim the truth for themselves, and collectively the Western churches have approached overseas mission alongside political expansion. Other faiths, other cultures, have been treated as uncivilised and brought within a western framework.

Even the French priest and scientist Teilhard de Chardin, a man sensitive to the riches of Chinese history, could write in 1923 'For long weeks I have been submerged in the deep flood of the people of Asia. And, now, as I come to the surface and collect my memories and impressions, I am forced to admit that in that direction too my quest has been in vain. Nowhere, among the men I met or heard about, have I discerned the smallest seed whose growth will benefit the future of man. Throughout my whole journey I found nothing but absence of thought, senile thought, or infantile thought.'[9]

The present state of the church is easily confused with the coming kingdom of God. In reaction, it is possible to be dismissive of the detail of ecclesiastical debate to reform liturgy or canon law, or impatient with the subtleties of ecumenical negotiation. Yet these may be vital for the self-understanding or well-being of the church. In addition, the propensity of human beings for self-deception is such that it is wise to question any spirituality that is not firmly rooted in a tradition of prayer, and practised in the life of a local church.

But churches can use power to avoid questions of truth. If adherence to a particular denomination is important so is the ability to listen to the experience of others and to be sharply critical of one's own denominational practice. Ecumenical and cross-cultural experience can provide an energy to challenge the partial witness of the local and denominational church.

In his ministry Alastair could see that the disunity of the churches in Scotland – and, in his earlier years their mutual antipathy - obscured the mission of Christ and reinforced social divisions and stereotypes in Scottish society. He committed himself to work for unity and was prepared for the slow negotiations, setbacks and breakthroughs characteristic of ecumenical dialogues.

Anyone deeply committed to the ecumenical task as part of the reconciling work of Christ has to accept that in growing towards visible unity, familiar patterns of church life will have to be relinquished. Denominational identity and history will be renegotiated as they become part of a larger communion. The forms of church life as we currently know them are penultimate, and subject to correction to align them more closely to the demands of the kingdom of God.

This can be taken in an evolutionary sense. Another interpretation is suggested by the practice of the Orthodox tradition in which the identity of the church is only given eschatologically. Denominations are under judgement as to how far they reflect the unity and diversity of the being of God. Some in their structures and ministries may emphasise a unity focused in the person of the priest to the detriment of the initiative of the people. Others such as the Quakers may show a diversity of gifts, but not recognise the need for one person to represent the unity of the local church.

St. Maximus the Confessor, the seventh century Byzantine theologian, writes in his Mystagogy, a meditation on the liturgy of the church. ' ... the holy Church of God will be shown to be working for us the same effects as God, in the same way as the image reflects its archetype. For numerous and of almost infinite number are the men, women and children who are distinct from one another and vastly different by birth and appearance, by nationality and language, by customs and age, by opinions and skills, by manners and habits, by pursuits and studies, and still again by reputation, fortune, characteristics and connections: all are born into the Church and through it are reborn and recreated in the Spirit. To all in equal measure it gives and bestows one divine form and designation, to be Christ's and to carry his name.'[10]

In the Eucharistic liturgy the Spirit is invoked to open up the people and gifts to the coming reign of God. In the Liturgy of St. John Chrysostom, after the words of institution, the priest remembers not only the Last Supper but also the Resurrection, Ascension, Enthronement and Second Coming of the Saviour. The implication is that in the Eucharist, not only the past events of creation and salvation are recalled, but the end of all things is already present.

One of the tasks of the ordained minister may be to undermine the pretensions of their own denomination and to create a liturgical and eschatological space for God. This should not be confused with a romantic revolt against the institutional. It is a space won through self-knowledge and the removal of illusions. It keeps alive what Donald MacKinnon described as 'the element of *receptivity* in hope', when 'what we hope for we acknowledge by hoping, to be in part outside our power'.[11]

There are hard political choices and necessary conflicts to preserve and change the patterns of church life in a period when all authority is thought to be suspect. But the ordained minister who plays a key role in the mediation of tradition within the compromises of history, is to look forward to the purification and vindication of that tradition in the life of the heavenly city.

Conclusion

Theological training and preparation for ordination has changed in the past 25 years. In the Anglican church women have been ordained and now make up to 40% of the intake at some colleges. The age profile of candidates has altered, with many more seeking ordination later in life. In consequence there are more married couples and children in the community that surrounds candidates in training, and in the Church of England there are now more people preparing for ordination through regional courses and local ministry schemes than in the Colleges.

The curriculum has also altered. Most colleges now have close links with a university, (and establishing strong links with New College was one of Alastair's achievements as Principal of Coates Hall), and most students now gain a university validated qualification. Pastoral Studies has moved from the periphery to the centre of the curriculum and has gained a new missionary emphasis. Integration between different branches of theology has a greater prominence, as has the process of reflection and assessment.

The theological climate has changed too. In the mid 1970's the liberalism exemplified by the *Myth of God Incarnate*[12] was questioning the belief of the creeds. In the year 2000 theologians talk of the end of liberalism. There is a new confidence in evangelicalism that is usually allied with biblical, doctrinal and moral conservatism. John Milbank[13] and the Radical Orthodoxy group offer a trenchant and wider ranging critique of both modernism and post-modernism from a neo-Augustinian and liturgical perspective.

This renewed confidence in theological tradition recognises that the community of faith can offer a critique of non-religious forms of thought. At the same time it can be a positivist assertion that poses an undifferentiated opposition of gospel and culture. The vulnerability that allows faith to emerge out of doubt and questioning is denied, and the spiritual ascesis of truth is short-circuited by fundamentalisms of text and structure.

But, even in changed times, some of the underlying aims of formation for ministry remain the same. How do students take root in the practice of faith and explore the interweaving of theological traditions that interpret that practice? How do students have the confidence to do theology in the context of other disciplines of knowledge and with an eye to the social context in which knowledge is produced? And how do students commit themselves to the Church while retaining an awareness of its provisional character?

Alastair Haggart showed a way of living with such questions with integrity. Offering models of authentic ministerial practice, lay and ordained, is the touchstone of faith and witness today.

Footnotes

[1] Levinas (trans. Aronowicz) *Nine Talmudic Readings* (Indiana 1990) p.30ff
[2] Faith and Order Paper 153 *Confessing the One Faith* (WCC 1991) p.3
[3] Robinson *On Being the Church in the World* (Mowbray 1977) p.26
[4] Tutu *The Rainbow People of God* (Doubleday 1994)
[5] Merton *On Peace* (Mowbray 1976) *The Asian Journal* (Sheldon 1975)
[6] Williams *Lost Icons* (T & T Clark 2000)
[7] Zizioulas *Being as Communion* (DLT 1985) p.224
[8] Faith and Order Paper 111 *Baptism, Eucharist and Ministry* (Geneva 1982) Ministry 8
[9] De Chardin *Letters from a Traveller* (Fontana 1967) p.59f
[10] Maximus the Confessor (ed. Berthold) *Selected Writings* (SPCK 1985) p.187
[11] Mackinnon *A Study in Ethical Theory* (Black 1957) p.255
[12] ed. Hick *The Myth of God Incarnate* (SCM 1977)
[13] cf. Especially Milbank *Theology and Social Theory* (Blackwells 1990)

The Changing Church and the Unchanging God

Michael Hare Duke

Theology has a problem with the language of eternity because it is trying to speak in the context of some particular time. When God is 'the Father of lights with whom is no variableness nor shadow of turning' (James 1,17) how does he engage with the actions and events of history and how do we describe the event? At one specific moment in time he took a human form. Luke in his Gospel is determined to pinpoint the exact dating of the occasions.

The census which brought Joseph and Mary to Bethlehem was 'when Cyrenius (Quirinius) was governor of Syria' (Luke 2,3). The start of John Baptist's ministry is even more meticulously dated 'In the fifteenth year of Tiberius Caesar's reign, when Pontius Pilate was governor of Judaea, Herod tetrarch of Galilee, his brother Philip tetrarch of the territories of Ituraea and Trachonitis, Lysanias tetrarch of Abilene, and while the high-priesthood was held by Annas and Caiaphas..'(Luke 3,1)

On these carefully dated occasions something happened of eternal significance. God was differently known. St. John gives an alternative reading, starting with the creation 'in the beginning'. Against that background the coming of the Christ is seen as giving a new significance to history. The miracles that he performs are 'signs' with a deeper meaning. The Cross is an unfolding of Passover, and as is made explicit in the Apocalypse, Jesus was 'the Lamb slain before the foundation of the world' (Rev. 13,8). The events were a way of unfolding what was already the case in the divine mind.

This overlapping of the theological categories makes for confusion when we are challenged by change to adapt either doctrine or church structures to meet new historical experiences. A classic example of this confrontation was when Galileo, as an empirical scientist, employed the new technology of telescopes to offer fresh evidence in favour of Copernicus' theory that the earth goes round the sun as opposed to the accepted mediaeval view that the universe was geocentric and that everything revolved around our planet. This was orthodox theology underpinned by Aristotelian philosophy. Behind this however lay the notion that truth was eternal and that there was no place for a challenge to it by scientific experiment. Similarly the idea that church structures might change was not entertained. This however may have had as much to do with the lack of appreciation of history as the link between the Church and the eternity of God.

Today we are acutely aware of the need for historical accuracy in any description of an earlier period. The charge of anachronism immediately suggests a lack of scholarship. This never troubled Shakespeare as he borrowed his plots from sources of earlier times. Equally there is evidence in the King James version of the Bible that the translators had no notion that their characters lived differently from themselves. For instance in the Book of Daniel, when Shadrach, Meshach and Abednego were thrown into the burning fiery furnace they were bound in 'their coats, their hosen and their hats' (Daniel 3,21) The New Jerusalem Bible translates the same passage 'their cloaks, trousers, headgear and other garments'. Other translations try to approximate to the original picture.

When we have recognised this background, we can make more sense of a baffling statement that appeared in the Prayer Book of 1549, and was repeated in 1662 and surprisingly in 1929. It comes in the Preface to the Ordinal 'It is evident unto all men diligently reading Holy Scripture and ancient authors, that from the Apostles' time there have been these Orders of Ministers in Christ's Church; Bishops, Priests and Deacons'. Contemporary scholarship would now allow no such thing.

There have existed in the Church orders of ministry to which sometimes titles of Bishop, Priest and Deacon have been applied, but with varying expectations of what their function might be. This becomes clear if we look at a description of a third century congregation at worship. The quotation is taken from a work by the liturgical scholar Dom Gregory Dix. He has set it in twentieth century terms to illustrate the difference between then and now. What also appears is the difference between New Testament times and two and a half centuries on.

> "Suppose you were a grocer in Brondesbury", he wrote "a tradesman in a small way of business as so many of the early Roman Christians were. Week by week at half-past four or five o'clock on Sunday morning (an ordinary working day in pagan Rome) before most people were stirring, you would set out through the silent streets with something in your pocket looking very like what we should call a bun or scone. At the end of your walk you would slip in through the mews at the back of one of the big houses near Hyde Park, owned by a wealthy Christian woman. There in her drawing room, looking just as it did every day, you would find the 'church' assembling - socially a very mixed gathering indeed.

A man would look at you keenly as you went in, the deacon 'observing those who come in', but he knows you and smiles and says something⊓ At the other end of the drawing-room sitting in the best arm chair is an elderly man, a gentleman by his clothes but nothing out of the ordinary - the Bishop of London. On either side of him is standing another man, perhaps talking quietly to him. On chairs in a semicircle facing down the room, looking very obviously what they are - a committee - sit the presbyters. In front of them is a small drawing-room table. The eucharist is about to begin".

(Dix Shape of the Liturgy, p 142)

Within a generation a radical change had taken place. In 312AD the Emperor Constantine won the battle of the Milvian Bridge and established the Christian faith as the religion of the Empire. This gave the Church a new status but also meant that the State had an interest in its governance. When the Arian controversy broke out, concerning the doctrine of Christ and how he was to be understood as both God and man, it became apparent to the Emperor that this was an explosive debate that could threaten civil order. He determined that it should be settled and the Council of Nicaea was convened: he presided over the assembled bishops and Imperial troops guarded the doors. Under these circumstances the formula which came to be known as the Nicene Creed was eventually evolved.

Bishops were now clearly established with a role at the Byzantine court and in the regions of the Empire. They were part of the power structures. This continued as the position of the Church was secured as a secular force, crowning kings and emperors and lending moral authority to the laws of the state. From such beginnings, through the court of

Charlemagne and on into the Middle Ages, bishops developed in parallel with the secular power of the barons.

John Moorman documented this development in his book, *Church life in England in the Thirteenth Century.* A bishop might have started his ministry in a religious order. John Pecham, Archbishop of Canterbury was a Franciscan friar but his life-style was almost by necessity that of a great landowner with extensive feudal rights and wide powers over both clergy and laity. This meant that the Crown had a special interest in their appointment and that bishops had a status which had to be maintained. A bishop's household was therefore composed of around forty members; clerics, legal officers, administrators of the bishop's estates and men at arms. So large a retinue could not find provisions at any one manor for more than a short time and therefore the diocesan was condemned to a nomadic existence. When it is remembered that many bishops were scholars who had enjoyed the advantages of a monastic library, the continual travelling must have seriously limited their time for reading and writing. As always it was the secular models of leadership that impinged on the way that the institution of the Church was organised. The life style of the barons had determined that of the bishops. By way of historical parallel it may be noted that the Reformed Church in Hungary which is a Calvinist foundation and therefore would be expected to have a Presbyterian polity, has in fact bishops. This was because in the time of the Austro-Hungarian Empire the court made it clear that it could not relate to the continuous circulation of Presbyterian moderators, but required permanently established bishops. As the result the Hungarian Reformed Church has bishops, even though its headquarters in Debrecen is known as the Geneva of the East!

When, in 1549 Cranmer in his First Prayer Book wrote the

service for the Consecration of a Bishop, it again reflected the political realities of the day. After the reading of the Gospel the presenting bishops introduce the candidate. The rubric which follows states

> *"And then the Kynges mandate to the Archebisshoppe for the consecration shall be read. And the othe touching the knowledging of the kings supremacie, shalbe ministred to the person elected*⎤*."*

Due obedience to the royal authority and the structured management of the church institution are also included in the questions to the candidate

> *"Are you persuaded that you be truly called to this ministration according to the will of our Lord and the order of this Realm?"*

The purpose of this call was to teach by word and example, to confound error and to evangelise. The bishop promised to base his teaching on scripture and to make this the authority for his ministry

> *"Are you persuaded that the holy Scriptures contain sufficiently all doctrine required of necessity for eternal salvation trough the faith of Jesus Christ? And are you determined with the same holy Scriptures to instruct the people committed to your charge and to teach or maintain nothing as required of necessity to eternal salvation but that you shall be persuaded may be concluded and proved by the same?*
>
> *Will you then faithfully exercise yourself in the said holy scriptures and call upon God by prayer for the true understanding of the same so as ye may be able*

by them to teach and exhort with wholesome doctrine and to withstand and convince the gainsayers?"

Church teaching and secular morality are perceived to overlap, the one reinforcing the other.

"Be you ready with all faithful diligence to banish and drive away all erroneous and strange doctrine contrary to God's word and both privately and openly to call upon and encourage other to do the same?

Will you maintain and set forward (as much as shall lie in you) quietness, peace and love. And such as be unquiet, disobedient and criminous within your diocese, correct and punish, according to such authority as ye have by God's word and as to you shall be committed by the ordinance of this realm?"

There is also a question which has a social rather than an ecclesial implication

"Will you shewe yourself gentle and be mercifull for Christ's sake to poore and needy people and to al straungers destitute of help?"

Because such powers are capable of abuse, there is a charge to the bishop that follows after the presentation of the Bible and then the Pastoral Staff. The Archbishop says

"Be to the flock of Christ a shepherd, not a wolf, feed them, devour them not, hold up the weak, heal the sick, bind together the broken. Bring again the outcasts, seek the lost: Be so merciful that you be not too remiss, so minister discipline that you forget not mercy: that when

97

the chief shepherd shall come ye may receive the immarcessible (in later versions 'never-fading') crown of glory"

In 1549 the service reflected the Church polity that was evolving under the Tudor monarchy. This is very different from the situation of a present day diocesan, and when still in use in the 1950s, before Prayer Book revision, made curious reading. The Prayer Book understanding of a bishop's role still found an echo in the culture of the nineteenth century where a bishop might still proceed against his clergy in the secular courts. Five cases including that of the Revd S.F. Green in the Diocese of Manchester and others in London, Birmingham, Liverpool, saw priests imprisoned for contempt of court over a charge of contravening the Ornaments Rubric. This was part of the controversy about eucharistic ritual. Individual Diocesan Bishops were embarrassed to be caught into a judicial role although the chief protagonists were the militantly anti-papal and largely lay-led Church Association. Archbishop Tait, right up to the time of his death, found himself acting as mediator in an attempt to reduce the scandal of a church at war with its clergy over what to the world appeared a very secondary issue. Once again the Church had absorbed into its models of leadership some of the assumptions that had evolved from both the experience of the French and Industrial Revolutions. One included an obsessive fear of any threat to the existing order and the other was the culture of the mill-owner who expected the lively co-operation of his work-force, but was threatened by any hint of trades union collaboration.

In the twentieth century the social context has changed still further. After the First World War the mood of docility which took troops over the top following their officers had gone. The stage was set for first a fresh look at democracy and then a shift to a society where people were the consumers and the leadership was accountable to them for quality and performance. The power lay not in the inherent authority of status but in the empirical ability to deliver what was wanted. In a way the Church has joined the rest of the shops on the High Street and customers come in to see if their wants are satisfied. For some it is The Old Curiosity Shop where they look for comforting memorabilia. For others it is like a Chinese restaurant where the dishes are mixed and matched to suit the taste of the individual liturgical palate: "1662 words, contemporary hymns with clapping, lay led intercessions. Or; modern language liturgy, guitar music, participatory sermon. Or; 1928 Prayer Book, songs of praise, anthology of intercession." The consumer rewards with his or her custom the shop which best satisfies the need.

The dynamics of this society are described in Berger's 'The Heretical Imperative'. His thesis is that once religion has abandoned the notion of one inerrant truth, faith is subject to 'choice' (in Greek haeresis from which is derived 'heresy'). We are in a market place where orthodoxy is displayed on one stall with no more claim to adherence than other brands of Christian belief or other world religions. The consumer evaluates and chooses.

This is in line with a society which has abandoned hierarchy and left the individual to make up his or her own mind on the basis of the conviction inspired by the exponent of a particular faith system. The consequences of this can be alarming. The inner authority of each individual is affirmed at the cost of any coherent pattern to which a whole society can make an appeal.

There is a wide-spread sense of spiritual malaise. This may be linked to the decline of any corporate belief. In spite of a general affirmation of some sense of the transcendent, increasing numbers of Christians are abandoning any church membership. What response might be appropriate from bishops who still retain a role as leaders of mission?

This issue has taken on a new urgency since the Lambeth Conference of 1998. Two powerful lobbies in the field of human sexuality are demanding support from bishops for their particular interpretation of Christian morality. Where they cannot find this, some are moving to the area of private judgement but others by contrast are endeavouring to set up alternative Episcopal arrangements. This a tortuous way of seeking validation for a private judgement by choosing the external validating authority on the basis of its known predetermined position.

"I will not accept A as my bishop because he disagrees with me and that impugns his lawful authority, but I will give such authority to B because he agrees with me" This is individualism run riot, but cloaking itself in institutional forms. It requires a rigorous sociological as well as a theological critique. Part of the present disarray may be manifest in the despair of those who might undertake such a task, fearing that only those who were predisposed to agree would accept any such analysis. Yet this is the death of rational discourse and shared morality, if every conclusion can be undermined by enquiring into why a person thinks that way or holds such an opinion.

Understanding and honouring the nature of truth lies at the heart of any coherent society. To make a preferred opinion more acceptable by cunning presentation, 'spin-doctoring', to undermine an opponent's point of view by an appeal to defects in his psychology, or exposing reasons why he needs to think that way, may at times be a way of addressing the variables in a particular debate, but in the last analysis, the logical deduction from what is the nature of the case must guide human reason in faith and action. A bishop is sometimes given the title of 'Guardian of the Truth'. Once this was assumed to mean that like a dragon outside a treasure store, his job was to protect the unchangeable riches of the faith once delivered to the saints. Are we now coming to a new interpretation of the bishop as the guarantor of an honest and truthful process of search; the servant of truth that is not a hard-edged artefact, but more like the developing relationship of love or a rainbow appearing in the clouds?

As we have seen across the centuries the social context of the church has changed, the model of operation has changed and the style of leadership has changed. There are no direct links between earlier days and our own except the misleading titles of the ministry. The one effective connection is the teaching, which determines the quality of the relationships between the members. Even there no specific codes of conduct apply, attitudes to slavery have, for instance, been revolutionised, the treatment of women has altered, so have family codes. Equally the understanding of physical disease has developed and so has the attitude to mental illness and consequently so have the patterns of treatment and the assumptions about what is appropriate.

A church which is to minister in a different environment has to be part of that environment and not be at odds with its self-understanding, or in disagreement with its intellectual assumptions. There are of necessity points at which it will come into conflict, but if there is no common ground, then engagement cannot take place. No sharing of insights, no evangelism is possible.

This issue was part of the debate at the Lambeth Conference

of 1988 under the title of Christ and Culture. It went unresolved and ten years later erupted in the bitter antagonism which left the bishops deeply divided under the party labels of Fundamentalists and Liberals. Much emotion was fed into the situation because the flash point was human sexuality, but the division was more fundamental. A serious look at history and a cool reflection on the variety of ways in which *episcope* is exercised in the church to-day might make for tolerance of the differences and help all parties discover what it means to talk of the unchanging nature of God.

A Case for Re-form:
Personal, Collegial and Communal

Mary Tanner

In each generation the Church has been faced with new challenges to its faith, order and moral life. Today is no exception. The Anglican Communion is not the only church to be threatened by questions of whether lay persons may preside at the eucharist, or women may be ordained to the priesthood, or whether homosexual partnerships are an acceptable lifestyle for those ordained to the priesthood. Every church struggles to understand how decisions that affect the communion of the Church should be taken, how a ministry of oversight should be exercised, and how unity is to be preserved in the face of deep differences of opinion. Many ecumenical conversations, both bilateral and multilateral, have considered what ministries of oversight would best serve the unity and maintain proper diversity, in a visibly united Church of the future. These are issues that Alastair Haggart, as a bishop in the Universal Church, a Primate of a province of the Anglican Communion, and a leader in the ecumenical movement, was not a little exercised by throughout his ministry.

One of the most useful insights so far offered for understanding the maintenance of communion and the exercise of oversight in the Church comes from the multilateral faith and order discussion with the introduction into the conversation of the triad, 'personal, collegial, and communal'. This essay traces the origins and development of the triad and explores some of the challenges this, at first sight cryptic formula, has for the current exercise of the ministry of oversight in the churches, and what hope it holds for a visibly united church in the future.

The first World Conference on Faith and Order met in Lausanne, in 1927. One of its 'certain suggestions as to possible church organisation', coming from a group working on the ministry of the Church, was:

1.   In view of the place which the episcopate, the council of presbyters, and the congregation of the faithful,respectively, had in the constitution of the early Church;

2.   And in view of the fact that episcopal, presbyterial and congregational order are each today, and have been for centuries, accepted by great communions in Christendom;

3.   And in view of the fact that episcopal, presbyterial and congregational order are each believed by many to be essential in the order of the Church, therefore, we must recognise that these several elements must all, under conditions which require further study, have an appropriate place in the order of life of a reunited Church, and that each separate Communion, recalling the abundant blessing of God vouchsafed to its ministry in the past, should gladly bring to the common life of the united Church its own spiritual treasures. [1]

The way in which this suggestion holds together the episcopal, presbyterial and congregational systems, seeing each of them as being 'essential' to the good ordering of the Church, had great potential. It was a challenge to divided churches, whose polities tended to overemphasise one or other aspect to the neglect of the others, to consider receiving complementary gifts from others. At the same time it offered, in embryonic form, a model for the structure of a visibly united Church in which the episcopal, the presbyterial and the congregational systems would be combined. Lausanne itself was clear that these different dimensions required further study.

This potentially creative insight of Lausanne of the triad, 'episcopal, presbyterial and congregational', together with other foundational work on ordained ministry, received almost no attention for thirty years. The emphasis passed, not surprisingly in view of the social and political changes taking place in Europe, to the ministry of the whole people of God, the royal priesthood, focusing on the search for 'the true doctrine of the laity'. But in 1963 the Fourth World Conference on Faith and Order, in Montreal, returned to the issue of the 'special ministry' and called for a study on the relation, and distinction, between the special ministry, as one gift among the many gifts, and the ministry of the whole people of God.[2] This led, 10 years later, to the publication of the Accra Report, *One Baptism, One Eucharist and a Mutually Recognised Ministry,* the report that was to develop into the most important ecumenical document of the century, the Lima Report, *Baptism, Eucharist and Ministry.*[3]

The Accra Report had little to say on the matter of *episkope* and made no reference to the triad, personal, presbyterial and congregational. As a result, the churches called for more work and a small consultation met in Geneva in 1979 to reflect on the ministry of oversight.[4] Among the five papers the meeting had to inform its work was one by the Orthodox theologian, John Zizioulas, on the evidence of the early church.[5] It was the paper by Zizioulas that was to determine the way things would develop.

Reflecting on the life of the early church, Zizioulas emphasised the close relation that there was between the exercise of *episkope* and the local eucharistic community. The community and the bishop (*episcopos*), surrounded by his presbyters, belonged together in the exercise of oversight. Collegial and conciliar gatherings were not structures over or above local communities that ignored or by-passed the community of the local church. Decisions were made in synods and councils by those who represented their local churches. Their decisions had to be received by the local communities in order for them to be fully valid. There was no idea of the subjection of passive laity to decisions made by a higher order. A ministry of oversight existed in the final analysis within the relational life of a concrete community. With the development of councils at the universal level, the presence at councils of bishops, whose life and ministry was inextricably bound up with local churches, meant that the exercise of oversight was always in relation to the local community, and in the service of the communion of the local churches. The presence of bishops of local churches at councils meant also that the unity of the Church passed through the bishops of local churches. The unity of the Church was about the unity of communities and not about the unity of individuals. The concern of early councils was not about promulgating right dogmas, but about the maintenance of the communion of the local churches.

These reflections on the life of the early church had an influence on the Memorandum issued by the Geneva meeting.[6] Responding to the question –How is *episkope* to be exercised in the Church? – the Memorandum concluded that *episkope* has three dimensions: personal, collegial and communal – echoing Lausanne's triad, personal, presbyterial and congregational. First, '*episkope* requires the authority and the commitment of single persons within the community. The presence of Jesus Christ in the midst of the people can best be witnessed to by one person proclaiming the Gospel and calling the community to witness and service. One person can provide an effective focus within the community and keep it in unity of life, worship and witness'. Secondly, personal *episkope* can only be carried out in a collegial way, for the authority of the one needs to be tested out by a group. The discovery of God's will requires the insights and interaction of several people. Finally, the Memorandum says,

> '*episkope* has a communal dimension. It is exercised not over the community but with the collaboration and participation of the community.' The Memorandum also pointed out that when the Ignatian model of the bishop, surrounded by his presbyters, in the local church gave way to the bishop exercising *episkope* over several eucharistic communities, and even larger areas, the three dimensions of *episkope,* the personal, collegial and communal applied to every level of the church's life.'

The triad was understood as offering a 'tool', or 'template', by which each church could test its own contemporary life. It was clear that 'in some traditions, the personal dimension of *episkope* currently eclipses the collegial and communal dimensions. In other churches, the personal ministry tends to be drowned in collegial and communal processes'. The ecumenical movement was seen as opening up the possibility of restoring the balance between the three dimensions. And there was the further implication that the restoration of balance should happen at the local, regional and international levels.

In picking up the triad from Lausanne and developing it in line with Zizioulas's paper on the early church, the foundation was laid for the section of the Lima Report - 'the guiding principles for the exercise of ordained ministry'. B.E.M. outlines the way that ordained ministry should be exercised in a 'personal, collegial and communal way'. A rationale for each dimension is given which echoes the words of the Geneva Memorandum:

It should be *personal* because the presence of Christ among his people can most effectively be pointed to by the person ordained to proclaim the Gospel and to call the community to serve the Lord in unity of life and witness. It should be *collegial,* for there is need for a college of ordained ministers sharing in the common task of representing the concerns of the community. Finally, the intimate relationship between the ordained ministry and the community should find expression in a *communal* dimension where the exercise of the ordained ministry is rooted in the life of the community and requires the community's effective participation in the discovery of God's will and the guidance of the Spirit.[7]

B.E.M. goes on to suggest that the ordained ministry should be constitutionally and canonically ordered, and exercised, in such a way that the three dimensions find adequate expression. At the level of the local eucharistic community, the ordained minister should act within a collegial body and emphasis should be put on the participation of all in the life and decision making of the church. At the regional level also there is need for an ordained ministry and the collegial and communal dimensions should find expression in regular representative synodal gatherings. Unlike the Memorandum, the paragraph makes no reference to the world level.

The ecumenical triad, personal, collegial, communal is essentially concerned with how Christians are enabled to live a life of belonging to one another in the communion of the Church, how they are to discover and live with one heart and mind. The triad refers to much more than the structural life of the Church. In the Church, the personal and relational dimensions of life are prior to the structural and organisational, but the personal and relational require the structural and organisational. Through the personal, collegial and communal exercise of oversight, Christians are kept in relationship to one another, both in the local church and in the communion of all the local churches. The local is the primary manifestation of the life of the Church, but needs a living relationship with all the local churches in order to be authentically the Church. The personal, collegial and communal dimensions of the Church are the means whereby the local church is connected to all the local churches. What the triad offers is a way for the Church to live as an interconnected, universal communion, and to live in such a way that the structural and institutional is always at the service of the personal and relational.

In the Church every individual counts as equal and each has a part to play in the exercise of oversight. Those set aside through ordination for a special ministry of oversight are placed within and among, and not over or above, the fellowship of the Church. They exercise that ministry in, with and among the local community they are called to serve. A bishop, or overseer, is only a faithful bishop or overseer in so far as that person is in close communion with the community. As the Orthodox theologian Nicholas Lossky expressed it, ' a bishop without a community is a skull, not a head; but a community without a bishop is a skeleton, not a body'. Those who are set aside to exercise oversight only do so faithfully when, by listening to the local community, they are able to voice the mind of the local community at collegial gatherings. And they only act in an authentically collegial way when they reflect back to the local community the mind of all the communities as that mind has been expressed in the collegial gathering of those who have been entrusted with a ministry of personal oversight.

The communal dimension is always present in the life of the Church. It is there in the relation with the community of the one with personal oversight. It is there whenever those with oversight gather together, taking with them into the collegial gatherings the hearts and minds of their local communities. It is there in councils and synods, where representative lay people focus the ongoing, day to day relationship that the one with personal oversight has with the community. The stress in the ecumenical discussion on the manifestation of personal, collegial and communal dimensions at every level of the Church's life, ensures that the local church is connected to the world-wide Church. The institutional and organisational life of the Church, whether at local, or at world level, is in the service of persons in communion with one another.

All ecumenical reports are 'ideal' and not 'actual'. They present a view of things as they ought to be, not as they are. For those who can hear, they imply that radical re-formation is needed in the life of every church. But after 60 years of ecumenical conversation it is apparent that few churches have grasped the radical nature of the ecumenical challenge, including the challenge that is there in the triad, personal, collegial and communal. When *Baptism Eucharist and Ministry* was sent to the churches in 1982 the churches were asked - could they recognise in the report 'the faith of the Church through the ages'; if so what challenges did this hold for the re-formation of their own lives; and what were the implications for their relations with other churches that could also recognise the same faith in the text? Almost every response devoted its entire attention to answering the first question. It is much easier, and far less threatening, to deal with disembodied theology, to reflect on the 'ideal' and to ignore the implications for the actual life of a church and its relations with others. Answers to the first question don't require costly repentance or conversion of identity. If the churches had really understood what was implied in the triad, personal, collegial and communal, then they would have recognised the need for renewal in their own lives, and for re-formation of their relations with other Christian communities.

First, if the personal exercise of oversight is to be truly relational, this requires that the person exercising oversight knows, and is known by, the local community he or she is called to serve. This has obvious implications for the size of a local church. If it is too large, the 'overseer' or bishop cannot listen to the community, nor represent its views in collegial gatherings, nor communicate the mind of all the local churches back to the community. As the Geneva Memorandum put it: 'when bishops are strangers to the congregations... the size of a diocese will require modification.'[8] This is certainly a challenge for the Church of England where the size of dioceses makes it hardly possible for a diocesan bishop to know, or be known, by the people in any effective way. The introduction of suffragan bishops is an anomaly and only confuses the personal-relational dimension of the ministry of oversight. It is hard to commend personal episcopacy to churches which do not have bishops, when the size of dioceses seems to magnify the office and to diminish the personal-relational aspect of that ministry. The Church of England, in spite of repeated calls to review the size of dioceses, remains oblivious to the way its own exercise of episcopacy distorts the credibility of the gift it has to offer others.

Secondly, if the personal -relational aspect of the ministry of oversight is to be more authentically lived out, then fresh thought needs to be given to what it means to be a representative person. What does it mean, both for those who are called to represent and for those who are represented? Without clarity about this there will be the temptation to think that everyone can, and should, do everything, that there are no distinctive functions.

A representative ministry implies mutual responsibility and mutual accountability. It implies responsibility of those chosen to represent the community, as well as responsibility of the community towards the one it has chosen to be its representative. Those who represent the community have a duty to listen to the community, to discern the mind of Christ in conversation with the local community, and in conversation with all the local communities. In listening to the community and reflecting back the mind of the community, special attention has to be given to those who are marginalised, those who find it hard to get their opinions heard. The range of opinion on any issue has to be faithfully considered and acknowledged. Being a representative spokesperson inevitably raises the question of how far a bishop, or overseer, is free to voice his, or her, personal opinions, and how far, he or she is to reflect the mind of the people at any given time. There is a delicate balance between the prophetic ministry of oversight and the role of being the representative of a local community. The scope, that those who have been chosen to represent have, to speak their own individual opinion when it is at odds with the mind of the community, or at odds with the mind of all local communities, is a difficult issue. A balance has to be maintained between the representative role and the leadership role of an overseer. There are examples today of churches where individual overseers are at odds with their local community. This was an issue explored by the house of Bishops of the Church of England in 1987. The view of the House was that bishops have to be sensitive both to traditional beliefs as well as to fresh insights.

A bishop may properly enter into questioning on matters of belief, both because as a man of integrity he will feel any force

112

there is in such questionings, and also because, as a leader, part of his responsibility on behalf of the church is to listen honestly to criticisms of its faith and life. But in all that he says he must take care not to present variant beliefs as if they were the faith of the Church: and he must always make as sure as he can that his hearers understand what that faith is and the reasons for it.

It is impossible to go far down the road of exploring what is entailed in representative ministry without returning to an issue raised in the Geneva Memorandum, but which had been dropped by the time of *Baptism, Eucharist and Ministry,* namely the place of women in the ministry of oversight. Bishop Oliver Tomkins once wrote that : 'If the essence of priesthood is to be the ministerial representative of the Church as the Body of Christ, can the total Christ be represented by less than the total humanity?' The same must surely apply to a ministry of oversight in the Church – a challenge to those churches that continue to exclude women from a personal ministry of oversight.

Thirdly, the embracing of a triad, built upon the primacy of the personal and relational life of the Church, requires churches to address issues of power and authority. The exercise of a ministry of oversight entails the exercise of power and authority. This is inescapable in any structured community. Power enables things to happen, it enables the community to live an ordered life, it is able to direct a response to new challenges, and galvanise the Church for mission. It is, however, evident that throughout history, and still today, power and authority have been used for selfish ends, for self-aggrandisement. Those with power and authority have often ridden rough-shod over individuals and groups that they were there to serve. The ecumenical emphasis upon the relational character of the ministry of oversight and the insistence that

113

it is Christ's authority that is lodged in the Church, ought to be a corrective against abusive use of power, but it will only be so if churches are willing to examine themselves and to own up to abuses of power. The Bishop of Rome has given a lead in *Ut Unum Sint,* where he acknowledges the existence of sinful structures as one of the causes of division in the Church.[9] At the beginning of a new millennium the Pope has asked forgiveness for the wrongs committed by members of the Church, including the Inquisition and the Crusades, but abuse of power is not only a thing of the past.

Fourthly, the triad continues to challenge churches whose polities overemphasise one aspect of the personal, collegial or communal dimension to the neglect of the others. Some churches are called to re-evaluate a personal ministry of oversight, as well as the exercise of collegiality. The Methodist Church, for example, has been looking at the role of District Chairmen, the Baptist Union of Great Britain the place of Superintendency and the Church of England's House of Bishops has recently considered the ministry of collegiality. On the other hand those churches whose polity, like that of the Roman Catholic Church, emphasises the personal and collegial, are challenged to consider how the communal dimension can restore a balance to the life of the church. Canonical legislation in the Roman Catholic Church now requires lay men and women to play a part in parochial and diocesan pastoral councils and diocesan synods. But this is slow in being put into practice and there is not a little cynicism among the laity who see little energy or enthusiasm for this to happen.

But understanding what is involved in the communal dimension is still far from clear. The triad is not primarily about structures. It is in the first place about the relational life of the Church. Nevertheless, it is often interpreted as having only a structural reference. The communal dimension tends then to be seen simply as the active participation of a few lay people in decision-making structures and regular, representative, synodical gatherings. The participation of the whole people is understood less and less in terms of their ongoing, day to day, relationship with the person who exercises oversight, and more about the representation of the few lay people in synodical structures. In this way a few are separated out and 'exalted' to positions above the rest. Their duty is too often interpreted as in some way to curb the power of those entrusted with personal oversight.

In the Anglican Communion there are those who call for more room to be given to the communal dimension at world level. They understand this in terms of the creation of a synod of ordained and lay representatives at the world level. This, rather than the collegial gathering of bishops at the Lambeth Conference, would become the place where decisions for the life of the Communion would be taken. For some, the communal dimension has come to be seen as a form of democratic government where all must be represented by category and everything decided by majority vote. This is, however, very far from the vision of the Geneva consultation summed up in the triad. The communal dimension was understood not primarily in terms of a structure in which representative laity took their seats, in order to control unscrupulous and dictatorial bishops. The communal dimension was, rather, a description of a dimension of the ongoing day to day life of the community, what the Anglican-Roman Catholic Commission refers to as 'synodality', the walking together on the way of the whole people of God.[10] The communal dimension was in the first place a description of life in communion, rather than a statement about the organisational structure of the Church. The communal describes a relationship lived out pre-eminently in the local eucharistic community, where listening and discerning are the way of life shared by the community with those who have oversight. That same communal dimension continues to be expressed when all those who exercise oversight in local communities gather, as representatives of their communities, to discern the mind of the Church, and the communal dimension continues with the taking back of what has been discerned in the college, for response and reception by the local communities. The communal dimension of *episkope* is much more inclusive, dynamic, and continuous a part of the Church's life. It cannot be reduced to a few members participating in infrequent synods, without distorting the communal life of the Church. This is not to argue that synods, in which ordained and lay act together, are not required for the well being of the Church. Synods are important. They focus visibly the relationship of the bishop to the local community, but they are not the most important aspect of the communal way of exercising oversight.

For almost all churches, the hint that the personal, collegial and communal belong to every level of the Church's life, contains a challenge. The churches springing from the Reformation developed alongside nation states and tended to develop in distinct nations. In many cases their structures hardly extend beyond the national, or regional, although there has been in more recent years a development in the sense of being members of a world communion, with loose organisational structures, but these are not ecclesial structures, intrinsic to the life of the Church. Such churches are challenged by the ecumenical triad to consider the advantage for unity in diversity that world instruments of oversight would offer.

For almost all churches the triad, with its insistence on the personal ministry of oversight at a world level, raises the issue of what sort of ministry of universal primacy would best serve the relational life of the Church. The Bishop of Rome's recent invitation to the churches, in *Ut Unum Sint,* to help him consider his ministry of primacy in the service of the unity of the Church is on any reckoning one of the most important ecumenical invitations of the ecumenical century.[11] The Anglican and Roman Catholic members of the Anglican-Roman Catholic International Commission were convinced that this ministry is a 'gift to be shared'. They were equally aware that that ministry would need to be re-shaped and re-formed if it is to be widely re-received. They also saw that there is a very real sense in which it needs to be re-received by the Roman Catholic Church itself. The Commission looked to the ministry of universal primacy being exercised 'in collegiality and synodality', a ministry of the *servus servorum,* a ministry that would help to uphold the legitimate diversity of traditions, strengthening and safeguarding them in fidelity to the Gospel. 'This sort of primacy' they said, 'will assist the Church on earth to be the authentic catholic *koinonia* in which unity does not curtail diversity, and diversity does not endanger but enhances unity.' ARCIC paints an attractive picture:

'He (a universal primate) will promote the common good in ways that are not constrained by sectional interests, and offer a continuing and distinctive teaching ministry, particularly in addressing difficult theological and moral issues. A universal primacy of this style will welcome and protect theological enquiry and other forms of the search for truth, so that their results may enrich and strengthen both human wisdom and the Church's faith. Such a universal primacy might gather the churches in various ways for consultation and discussion.[12]'

But this is another 'ideal' ecumenical document. However attractive the thought of a personal focus of unity at the world level is, (someone who can call the local churches together), any positive response to such a ministry will depend upon the ability of the Church of Rome to re-form and re-model the exercise of universal primacy.

There is a final challenge implied in the ecumenical triad. If the exercise of oversight is truly relational, at every level of the Church's life, then decision making will inevitably be a lengthy, on-going process. Discovering the mind of Christ for the whole Church will entail drawing the whole community into the discernment process. Challenges which arise in a local church and which affect the unity and communion of the whole church will never be solved quickly. Differences will have to be made room for and lived with. Discernment needs space and time for the local insight to be tested in the communion of all the churches. Time has to be given for the *sensus fidei* to be discerned in the synods of the Church and the 'echo' heard back from the people. This requires of the whole Church a patient understanding of the processes of reception through which the mind of Christ for the Church is discovered. It requires the right relationship of those with oversight and the whole Church. As Nicholas Lash writes, the *sensus fidei* guides the whole Church, bishops and people alike, towards what Newman called that "deliberate judgement, in which the whole Church at length rests."[13] The ecumenical triad provides a skeletal structure that would provide for such a process.

'Personal, collegial, communal at every level of the Church's life', sounds like a cryptic, ecumenical formula, offering at best an ideal picture of a monolithic Church. But, when its origin is traced, and some of the thinking that lies behind it recovered, it is seen to contain important insights for how Christians could live together and face new issues which threaten the unity of the fellowship. It suggests what churches have to learn and receive from one another. It also offers in embryo a convincing guide for the life and structure of a visibly united Church in the future. Whether the churches are prepared to face the challenges and respond with re-form and re-newal in their own lives, or whether they are prepared to embody the insights in any new partnerships which they enter on the ecumenical journey, remains to be seen. The bishops at the 1998 Lambeth Conference committed the Anglican Communion to a goal of visible unity that included the embodiment of the personal, collegial and communal dimensions at every level of the Church's life. Whether the bishops understood the radical nature of that commitment, or have the will to respond to it, remains to be seen. What is sure is that Alastair Haggart himself would have understood those challenges, supported reformation in the life of the Anglican Communion, and the development of new ecumenical partnerships on the way to the visible unity of the Church.

Footnotes

1. *Proceedings of the World Conference on Faith and Order, Lausanne, 1927, London, SCM Press 1927, p.379*
2. *One Baptism, One Eucharist and a Mutually Recognised Ministry,* F and O Paper No 73, WCC, Geneva, 1975
3. Baptism, Eucharist and Ministry, F and O Paper No. 111, WCC, Geneva 1980
4. Episkope *and episcopate in ecumenical perspective,* F and O Paper 62, WCC, Geneva 1980
5. Episkope and Episcopos in the Early Church: A brief survey, ibid.p.30ff
6. ibid. p.1ff
7. *Baptism, Eucharist and Ministry,* M. para 26
8. ibid.p.11
9. Encyclical Letter of the Holy Father, John Paul II, *On Commitment to Ecumenism, Ut Unum Sint,* St Paul Books and Media, Boston, 1995
10. *The Gift of Authority, Authority in the Church III, An Agreed Statement by the Anglican-Roman Catholic International Commission, CTS, 1999*
11. ibid., para. 95
12. ibid., para. 60
13. Lash, N., *Waiting for the Echo,* in *The Tablet,* March 4, 2000

And the Truth Shall Set You Free

Martin Conway[1]

In the Gospel according to John, chapter 8 and verses 31/2, Jesus says: 'If you stand by my teaching you are truly my disciples; you will know the truth and the truth shall set you free.'

We will all readily agree that a university is centrally concerned with truth. Its many departments and courses are busy exploring, communicating, enlarging the complexes of truths they are variously handling, and thus broadening the powers of understanding, and the skills by which to use, these many truths. Truths by now so many, so diverse, so complex that no one person can possibly master them all.

Jesus spoke rather of 'the truth', a term which some people in universities today reject as meaningless in face of the ever-widening diversities of the many truths we deal with in our separate disciplines. Yet we cannot afford to dismiss the possibility of *truth*, in the singular, that recalls us to the centrality of what we *are* - human beings gifted with the ability to distinguish between truth and falsehood; and of what we *are for* - growing into the deeper and wider horizons of truth that our creator has enabled us to explore, respect and enjoy as a single, if highly complex, family of humankind.

In turn that points to the meaning of the proud title; 'university'. This is usually understood as an institution that deals - as nearly as possible - with the total range of knowledge, all the relevant subjects and disciplines, since these are in principle the same for all humankind, to whichever of our many languages, races, cultures or religious traditions any particular person or group may belong.

Yes indeed, but does that claim to universality in practice lead to a purposeful concern for the wholeness of truth, for a depth and singleness of outlook that will enable us to know how to handle the unknown and unpredictable realities and challenges with which life will face us? A university is surely cheating its students, and neglecting one of the key disciplines for its teachers, if no care is taken over what can bind them together in a common framework of purpose and commitment.

A year ago today I was in Harare, in Zimbabwe, for the 8th Assembly of the World Council of Churches[2]; a gathering of some 5000 people from most of the nations and cultures of humankind, assembled in the name of the truth entrusted by Jesus to his world-wide church - even if the all too many separated churches have done their fair bit to mishandle that truth over the centuries. That assembly, largely ignored by the media in this country, identified the central challenge now facing humankind as the growing gulf between rich and poor which so many of the powers that dominate our world seem literally hell-bent on increasing.

The programme of 'modernisation', for example, of our present New Labour government has been analysed in a recent lecture by the General Secretary of the Fabian Society[3] as resting on three pillars, three dominant processes driven by powers of this present age:

- the *globalization* that is forcefully integrating the world's economies and sweeping through the world's cultures. This is widely understood to arise from what is known as 'the Washington Consensus', that dates from the time when Ronald Reagan and Margaret Thatcher took the reins of power

122

respectively in the U.S.A. and U.K. and imposed first on to their own countries and eventually on to the world scene an ideology centred on the 'free market' of goods and of the movement of finance capital. This approach, driven by the so-called 'knowledge economy' that relies on both the rapid new communication technologies and the ever more rapacious application of entrepreneurial creativity, has by now captivated most of the institutions that claim to serve the world as a whole, not least the International Monetary Fund and World Bank, and is often taken for granted as the necessary basis of any international 'order'.

- the *individualisation* by which each of us comes to her or his own choices and decisions, with dwindling levels of attachment to any particular family or society or tradition. It is harder to pinpoint any specific starting date for this, but it has developed over many generations to a point that in North America and Europe now feels irreversible. Yet no great awareness of other cultures is needed to notice how much thinner and less reliable ours has become, precisely because one can never rely on any one else's judgment being taken for more than a personal opinion. The Chinese sense of family, for instance, or the way all 'indigenous' and 'aboriginal' peoples follow a strict communal discipline in their use of the land, alike reveal a very different approach to human relationships than that of 'modern' individualism. In the West, our identities and aspirations have become primarily geared to our chosen pattern of consumption, rather than to any sense of an interdependent life with and for others.

- the *inequality* that results from the primacy given to economic competition in a 'free' market. This also affects whole continents, nations, regions within a nation and areas or communities within a single town; it produces the gulf between those 'at the top' who reap the benefits and those 'at the bottom' who pay the real costs, and grows hour by hour, by the apparently unstoppable working of almost all the social and economic mechanisms which we who are at the top take for granted as unchallengeably 'normal'.

Jacobs maintains that the New Labour government has accepted all three of these 'approaches' as both inevitable and necessary, as basics that cannot and should not be challenged, even if at points they seem to stand for approaches directly opposed to the classic concerns of the Labour movement: hence the vigour, and at times the harshness, of Blair's insistence on 'New Labour'.

Given that a university has the potential to be a major force in countering these pillars and processes; how can it assist us in squaring up to the vast threats which these approaches pose to the future of mankind and to the finite resources of our planet? In each case, I suggest, we need to help one another to see beyond a half-truth which can easily dominate with its idealogical power, both our minds and our behaviour.

In regard to the *inequalities built into our economic systems*, economists will tell us that there is no alternative to the 'market' for ensuring the best distribution of scarce resources. The less regulated the market, the more commercially effective. But that half-truth says absolutely nothing about the human value of the resources on offer: should those who construct lethal land-mines be free to sell them in any corner shop ? Still more, it leaves out of account the sinews of human community; the love of parents for children, the friendships in which we help one another, the trust by which an army commander relies on support from his colleagues further down the line, the delight of an orchestra's violins responding to a peremptory call from the trombones. These cannot be counted in money values. The usefulness of markets, indeed of money, can only truly be measured within a framework of commitments and disciplines that rest more centrally on the possibilities of collaboration, indeed of mutual respect and love, than on competition and greed.

So too, in respect of *individualisation*. While all of us in a university have reason to enjoy the greater freedom of individuals who can look beyond their own family, culture or religious tradition, we are in consequence challenged to pursue our studies and reach our decisions mindful of the larger and properly social horizons of intentions and purposes that concern humankind as a whole, not just those of one person or one particular company or community. In Zimbabwe we learned a lot about the African world-view of 'ubuntu' - 'I am as I am because you are as you are and we all belong together', a way of seeing the world through the interweaving relationships in and for which we all grow up into contributing adults within and for the sake of the total human community. Friendship is a higher skill than entrepreneurship; love matters more to our common future than money.

In respect of *globalisation*, while we can only be glad that our world is now integrated to the point that we can send e-mails around the globe within seconds, can travel and share in many different ways with friends and neighbours from many nations; that friendship and partnerships, let alone any sense of human community, will be distorted if seen only in terms of the gains and rivalries of trade: the other and larger truth is that its primary value is found in enjoying one another's diverse cultures, serving each other's growth and being enriched by each other's different understandings and approaches. Last month's issue of *News from the New Economy*[4] warns that the real danger to be faced up to in the current W.T.O. meeting in Seattle is not that of globalization *per se* so much as the monoculture, the destruction of the variety of our human institutions and interests, the many socio-diversities that correspond to the fertile bio-diversities of our tropical forests. Multinational corporations totally fixated on money-driven competition on the global scale are in danger of turning the human race into the sort of 'melting pot' in which lowest common denominators drive out the God-given diversities that are among our most valuable gifts to one another.

So I rejoice that our worship today in this grandiose cathedral is a sign that the City University wants to take *the single and whole truth* Jesus was speaking about at least as seriously as *the many different and competing truths* that fill its more ordinary days. In saluting those who have successfully completed their courses and in honouring four people who have contributed richly to the life of both City and University, we will do well to ponder also on the mysterious, never wholly understood promise that Jesus here held out to his disciples and holds out today anew to all who can have ears to hear ...

> 'If you stand by my teaching you are truly my disciples; you will know the truth and the truth shall set you free.'

Footnotes

[1] Revision of an address delivered at the City University's Graduation Day Service, St Paul's Cathedral, London, 6th December 1999

[2] On which I have written a personal account *Journeying Together Towards Jubilee,* available from me at 303 Cowley Road, Oxford OX4 2AQ

[3] *Environmental Modernisation - The New Labour Agenda* by Michael Jacobs (Fabian Pamphlet 591, pp.49, ISBN 0 7163 0591 7, £5.00, available from The Fabian Society, 11 Dartmouth St., London SW1H 9BN). For his discussion of the points I mention here see especially pp. 14-20. This is the same Michael Jacobs who wrote / edited the invaluable *The Politics of the Real World* before the 1997 General Election for the 'Real World Coalition' of British NGOs (London: Earthscan, 1996, pp.146, £6.99, ISBN 1-85383-350-9).

[4] The monthly broadsheet of the New Economics Forum, available from NEF at Cinnamon House, 6-8 Cole St., London SE1 4YH.

"One Bread, One Body" Revisited[1]

John Fitzsimmons

It was Alastair Haggart who first, in his own eloquent fashion, explained to me the pain of those who share with the Roman Catholic Church a strong eucharistic faith of an 'objective' kind, and who yet are forbidden to approach the Sacrament in the Roman Church, even though they practise an 'Open Table' themselves.

It is not that I had never thought about it; it is simply that it had never been personalised for me, especially by one whom I had come to respect and admire and whose theological acumen I was just beginning to appreciate.

Ever since, I have looked at the question of intercommunion much less dispassionately. In fact, the problem has been to keep a sense of balance and to appreciate the arguments on both sides.

At the time we were in the middle of a dialogue which produced in due course "The Ecclesial Nature of the Eucharist. A Report by the Joint Study Group of Representatives of the Roman Catholic Church in Scotland and the Scottish Episcopal Church" (Glasgow 1973). Significantly, the Report ends with a Final Statement which includes this:

> "It is in our conversations centring on the relationship between the Eucharist and the Church that we have felt ourselves breaking new ground and moving closer to the heart of all ecumenical endeavour. Not only have we been able to reach a degree of agreement in this

context, but we have been able to see as a result the way in which our future discussions must go: the way is clear for us to open up the topic of the Ministry and ultimately of Intercommunion. ... It will be remembered that our study of the Eucharist in relation to the Church has meant that we had to discuss the Church's inner nature, its structure and its mission, as well as the connexion between the Eucharist and membership of the Church. From the fact that we recognise the connexion between the Eucharist and membership of the Church, it follows that we must consider this connexion in relation to the vexed question of intercommunion .... Throughout our work we have been activated by a desire to hasten the time when all Christians will be gathered in a common celebration of the Eucharist into that unity of the one and only Church which Christ bestowed on his Church from the beginning" (Vatican II: Decree on Ecumenism, Ch. I, no. 4 pp.24-25.

There are two points to be made here:

Firstly, in those days there did not seem to be any difficulty about members of churches describing themselves as 'representatives' of their respective bodies. Clearly, over the years, the churches have become much more cautious in this regard. Perhaps it is because people have come to see the sometimes radical implications of genuine ecumenical dialogue in depth; many have taken 'cold feet' as a result. Without doubt, many of the people in positions of 'authority' (or perhaps 'power' would be a better description) in the churches have seen those implications, and so brakes have been applied, structures have been put in place to make sure that any ecumenical movement proceeds, like the proverbial convoy, 'at the speed of the slowest'.

Secondly, however, it is clear that from the very start there were those who saw the real issues in ecumenism: the nature of the Church, the mutual recognition of ministries, and (above all) the recognition of one another at the Lord's Table. There was a lot of talk about relatively innocuous subjects like Baptism (though even in that area there were anomalies to be cleared up, such as the fact that the Roman Catholic Church in England and Wales recognised the baptism of the Church of Scotland whereas the Roman Church in Scotland apparently did not); in retrospect, it seems clear that people felt that they had to start somewhere and that 'safe' subjects were best attended to first. With the advent of A.C.T.S., many people warned that any attempt to re-invent the ecumenical wheel would be resisted, and yet the distinct impression is still abroad that A.C.T.S. has yet to grasp the central, 'neuralgic', issues.

Alastair Haggart was filled with a kind of 'divine impatience' – he was forever wanting to move things along, sometimes at the risk of not taking everyone with him, including some of his own; indeed, in many ways, my own shared experience with him was my introduction to a basic element of ecumenical work: you can find people from other traditions infinitely more congenial theologically than the people from your own church. Charming, witty, urbane, he yet possessed a degree of steel which could lead people down a golden path with dreamy vistas to match, and then he would suddenly confront his 'fellow pilgrim' with the implications, sometimes to their horror and very often to their downright fright.

Such was his approach to the question of intercommunion. He was impatient with a seeming unwillingness to take up the discussion; he was impatient with people who simply repeated tried and trusted formulae; he was thoroughly impatient with people who did not, or did not want to understand the acuteness of the 'pain of separation' experienced by so many who were filled with the desire to share with all their brothers and sisters in Christ the fullness of communion in the Body and Blood of Christ.

What is offered here is something that he would have approved of: as he used to say: "You have to keep picking away at it" and "the one thing you need is perseverance, which is a polite term for what I really mean, namely 'bloody-mindedness'". The churches seem to have retreated into the laager on the matter of intercommunion: the Roman Catholic Church, on the one hand, having restated its classic, 'traditional' position, and the other churches (with weary resignation all too often) simply letting it go at that for the sake of keeping some kind of dialogue going. Theirs is a charitable, not to say heroic, stance; whether the Roman authorities in any way appreciate it is a matter for some doubt.

"'Intercommunion' is one of the most acute 'neuralgic points' of the entire ecumenical dialogue. There has always been a great deal of concern about this topic, but increasing contacts between churches have made the question all the more pressing. It is a question which will not go away. With each ecumenical gathering, solemn or simple, with each inter-church marriage that is celebrated, with every step that is taken in genuine dialogue, it presses hard for an answer. The reasons for this are obvious: first and foremost, there is an instinct of grace within all Christians which wishes, above all else, to share the Table of the Lord with the rest of the believing community. Secondly, there is a sense in which all Christians use such sharing of the Eucharist as the measure of mutual recognition."[2]

Those are the opening sentences of a study document of the Unity, Faith and Order Commission of A.C.T.S. put together in 1994. The title is a giveaway: 'Intercommunion: the Churches Agree and Disagree'. The reason for that is fairly simple; it was merely the restatement of entrenched positions. The impasse it brings to our attention has not been resolved yet; in fact, it is a question if there is really the 'political will' to resolve it – at least if the body of statements made by the Roman Catholic Church (at a variety of levels) is anything to go by.[3] The parameters seem to be these: on the one hand, there is the classic Roman position which insists that sharing in the Eucharist is the sign of full communion with the Church, the Church in this instance being the Roman Catholic Church itself in union with the Bishop of Rome as its visible head. At a much deeper level, the real fundamental principle of the Roman position is a particular understanding of the nature of the Church itself, to the extent that the Eucharist and the Church are tied together and an acceptance of the Roman Catholic understanding of 'Church' is a prerequisite for admission to the sacraments of the Church, above all the Eucharist. The so-called 'Ecumenical Directory'[4] puts the matter quite fairly and succinctly: "eucharistic communion is inseparably linked to full ecclesial communion and its expression". This, at least, has the virtue of honesty: it states quite clearly the classic position that the sharing of the Eucharist is the end and summit of the quest for Christian unity; it is only when the Church is held together in unity – structural, organisational, doctrinal, and gathered together under the jurisdiction of the Pope. Every eucharistic prayer in the Roman Church is prayed in communion "with N. our Pope and N. our bishop". It was this that prompted Cardinal Schönborn, the present archbishop of Vienna to formulate his 'Simple Rule'. In essence, what it comes to is this: if anyone can assent to the notion of papal authority over the Universal Church and recognise the principle of episcopacy, then they might be admitted to communion in the Roman Church. The casual observer will immediately recognise the problem with this: there are those who for entirely conscientious (not to mention sound exegetical) reasons will resist the principle of episcopacy; there are many more who will find the 'high papalism' of the notion of the Pope's universal jurisdiction totally unacceptable. John Paul II himself has recognised the difficulty such a notion poses.[5] It may be added that there are not a few theologians in the Roman Catholic Church itself who find such an idea lacking in proper biblical and theological foundation. Brave as the cardinal of Vienna may be, it has to be admitted that he has not addressed the essence of the problem and that is the bond between ecclesiology and sacramental theology in much Roman Catholic thinking and writing.

For most, that bond has become like the bond of marriage – indissoluble. In other words, the theology of the Eucharist is so tied to the theology of the Church that it is quite unthinkable that they could be separated. Hence, for instance, 'One Bread One Body' has this to say:

> "The Church is most fully and visibly itself when it gathers for the Eucharist. There the Church expresses what it already is by God's gift, and what it must more truly become – a community of faith and love, one in Christ, holy by the power of the Spirit, catholic in the integrity of its faith and the universal scope of its outreach, apostolic in its living continuity with the faith and mission of the apostles and the Church throughout the ages. This communion with the Church across continents and centuries is a communion in the Spirit, but 'made flesh' in a visible way, above all in the Eucharist and through the bishops and priests who

preside at the Eucharist. This teaching is central to the Catholic understanding of the Church. The intimate link between the Church and its celebration of the Eucharist will be an essential point to remember when it comes to thinking about the meaning of receiving Holy Communion" (no. 19, p.6).

There are several remarks that have to be made in this connexion:

- What is said is commonly said, and in this instance very beautifully put. In our own way, we had said something similar in 'The Ecclesial Nature of the Eucharist':

> "Since the Church is the sign of Christ's saving action in the world and the means of that saving action, it lives at two levels. Its inner life and its structure are revealed in the Eucharist. It is here that we can see the need for holding two aspects of the Church in a dynamic tension. The Church is the visible society founded on the apostles, and at the same time the mystery of salvation always present ... THE EUCHARIST IS THE MYSTERY OF SALVATION CONSTITUTING THE CHURCH IN ITS INMOST BEING – THE PEOPLE OF GOD GATHERED TOGETHER IN THE UNITY OF THE FATHER, THE SON, AND HOLY SPIRIT" (p.20).

However, there is a certain sense of unease about the way all of this is stated as if it were immediately self-evident. Clearly, for many people of other traditions, it is not so clear. The implication has always been: this is the Catholic view (not just Roman Catholic) embraced by all the churches which consider themselves 'catholic', such as the churches of the East and those of the Anglican Communion. But, there can hardly be a mainstream church anywhere that does not think of itself as part of the 'Catholic Church' which we profess in the Apostles' Creed. It seems, then, that the tie-up between the notion of the Church and its inner structure and the Eucharist is not at the centre of every 'Catholic' consciousness, even though there is a fierce attachment to the idea of 'catholicity'. The phenomenon of *frükatholizismus* has always been dangerous territory in that many used it for ideological purposes on the one side and on the other. The balance is best struck by John Knox in 'The Early Church and the Coming Great Church' (Nashville 1955):

> "Although the situation of AD 200 did not exist in New Testament times, there were pointers in its direction; the several features of Catholicism cannot be understood simply as *ad hoc* responses to the threats of Gnostic heresy and the state's hostility, but were anticipated in, and in a degree fulfillments of, tendencies already present in the New Testament Church" (pp.114-115)".

It is a giant leap from that to the 'Catholic' vision developed over centuries by the Roman Church; the reference in the text to 'bishops and priests' is something of a 'lifting of the veil'. The essence of the discussion switches from sacramental theology to considerations of hierarchy, authority, jurisdiction, and (ultimately) power. It is a much smaller leap from this type of reflection to the rules and regulations for admission to the Sacrament, because the focus has shifted; the 'communion' which is under scrutiny is not 'communion with the Lord' but 'communion with the Church', and not only that but 'communion with the Church in its Roman Catholic manifestation' with all which that entails.

- The impression is sometimes given that the Roman Catholic Church has always had a univocal view of the Eucharist. It does not require too profound a sense of history to realise that this is simply not true. At one time, the whole point was to emphasise the relationship between the Eucharist and the Cross; hence, the whole theology of 'the Eucharist as Sacrifice' was excogitated.[6] Then the focus became the 'Real Presence', which gave rise not only to the phenomenon of 'Bleeding Corporals' (as in Bolsena) but also to the wonderful texts of Thomas Aquinas for the feast of Corpus Christi.[7] However, the spiritual and overtly religious side of this discussion was rapidly overtaken by the philosophical. The fact that the great Scholastic writers from Albert the Great onwards had 'baptized Aristotle' meant that the reflection on the real presence was carried forward in philosophical terms, to the extent that there was a risk of the Church's tying itself to one philosophical explanation, namely 'transubstantiation'[8] It is only in more recent times, that the Church of Rome has come on to an 'even keel' and has brought together the twin ideas of the Eucharist as Sacrifice and the Eucharist as Sacred Meal (in 'remembrance' of the Last Supper). The decree 'Sacrosanctum Concilium' (4.12.1963) of Vatican II on the Sacred Liturgy strikes the balance:

> "At the Last Supper, on the night when He was betrayed, our Saviour instituted the Eucharistic Sacrifice of His Body and Blood. He did this in order to perpetuate the sacrifice of the Cross throughout the centuries until He should come again, and so to entrust to His Beloved Spouse, the Church, a memorial of His Death and Resurrection: a Sacrament of Love, a Sign of Unity, a Bond of Charity, a Paschal Banquet in which Christ is consumed, the mind is filled with grace, and a pledge of future glory is given to us. The Church, therefore, earnestly desires that Christ's faithful, when present at this Mystery of Faith, should not be there as strangers

137

or silent spectators. On the contrary, through a proper appreciation of the rites and prayers they should participate knowingly, devoutly and actively. They should be instructed by God's Word and be refreshed at the Table of the Lord's Body; they should give thanks to God; by offering the Immaculate Victim, not only through the hands of the priest, but also with him, they should learn to offer themselves too. Through Christ the Mediator, they should be drawn day by day into ever closer union with God and with each other, so that finally God may be all in all." (ch.II, nos. 47-48).

In the aftermath of the Council, there was a great howl of protest in certain quarters that the teaching of the Council of Trent (1545-1563) had been betrayed. In fact, there is a very good case for suggesting that Vatican II merely said more clearly what Trent was trying to say, given that Trent was limited in its scope and addressed itself simply to what it regarded as the errors of the Protestant Reformation. Depending on the perspective, the whole Tridentine phenomenon is regarded as either the 'Counter Reformation' or the 'Catholic Reformation', and there are still those abroad in the Roman Catholic Church who regard its decrees as the ultimate flowering of the Faith, the definitive statement of what Catholicism is all about. Like many another ecumenical council, Trent never quite got to finish its agenda: those were difficult, warlike times, and no one was more warlike than the Papacy. It is interesting to compare the agenda of Trent on the theology of the Eucharist and that of Vatican II: it is as if nothing had happened in the intervening four hundred years.

Trent had on its agenda the use of the vernacular (*lingua vulgares*) in the celebration of Mass; it is one of the many things that did not reach the council-floor; political unrest and upheaval saw to that. But, the point is worth making: given time, Trent might have produced a more open, tolerant and 'modern' Church than actually came forth. The Protestant Reformers and their successors fully expected to be invited. All of this takes us into the realm of 'might have beens'; even Hubert Jedin, the great historian of Trent[9] used to wax eloquent on what 'might have been' if Trent had been called twenty, even ten, years earlier. As with the question of 'justification'[10] the impression is left that most of the theological to-ing and fro-ing on the subject of the Eucharist was really a matter of language and communication. Perhaps that is at least part – if not all – of the problem at the present time. Over the years since the Reformation, the Roman Catholic tradition and the Reformed Tradition have developed their own distinctive forms of discourse. The 'trick' has been to find a 'common language'; there are signs that it is emerging, but it has not been fully fashioned yet.

For Roman Catholics, and for all those who try valiantly to grasp what the Roman Church is trying to say, the decree 'Unitatis Redintegratio' (21.11.1964) of Vatican II must remain a point of reference. There is one major corrective to be introduced: the decree refers to 'churches' and 'ecclesial communities'; the criterion for using the two terms was that some groups were perceived to be closer to the 'ideal' of the Church (embodied, of course, in the Roman Catholic Church itself) such as the churches of the East. A somewhat specious rationale was given, namely that there are Christian communities which do not like to be designated as 'churches' as such. They must, surely, be few and far between – if indeed they exist at all. Over the years, this language has tended to disappear, but disappointingly still features in far too many Vatican documents, not least the 'Ecumenical Directory'[11] Vatican II expresses – and expresses well – the idea of the common sharing of the Eucharist as the summit of the ecumenical 'climb'; it is the point of the whole exercise, the 'Holy Grail' in more ways than one. The formula of *'Unitatis Redintegratio'* is a reprise of the Constitution on the Liturgy: "... little by little, as the obstacles to perfect ecclesiastical communion are overcome, all Christians will be gathered, in a common celebration of the Eucharist, into that unity of the one and only Church which Christ bestowed on His Church from the beginning" (*UR*, ch.I, no. 4). Taken in conjunction with the close tie-up between the idea of the Church and the idea of the Eucharist, intercommunion looks like the earthly equivalent of the Second Coming: something to look forward to, but presaging the 'end of the world' and ushering in a new 'Kingdom of God'.

THAT IS, UNTIL WE START LOOKING AT THE QUESTION OF EXCEPTIONS.

In the light of all of the foregoing, it might be imagined that there are no exceptions: the connexion between Church and Eucharist is so close that they cannot be separated. And yet, historically, right from the start, exceptions were being made; it is almost as if ecclesiology had overtaken the ecumenical considerations and the sacramental theology. The implications of what the Roman Church had to say about other Churches made it imperative that the exceptions be spelt out. Clearly, the Eastern Churches are in a class by themselves, since they are regarded by Rome as 'sister' churches. The fact that any kind of ecumenical dialogue between Rome and the Churches of the East has broken down does not affect the principle: they are regarded as having a true 'Catholic' sense of the Eucharist.[12] With regard to the 'Other Churches', there is clear enough principle: 'in general', the Roman Church only admits those who are in communion with the Bishop of Rome; but, there may be access to the Sacraments (Eucharist, Penance, and Anointing of the Sick) 'in certain circumstances', 'by way of exception', and 'under certain conditions', permitted, 'or even commended', for Christians of other Churches and ecclesial communities.[13] There really is no need to go into all of the 'circumstances' or 'exceptions', or 'conditions'. The point seems to be clear – the umbilical cord between Eucharist and Church has been cut, not by the maverick theologians or freelance rebellious clergy, but by the dicasteries of the Holy See itself. The logic seems clear: if there are exceptions, then the connexion between Eucharist and Church is not an absolute; if it is not an absolute, then there may well be another way of looking at the entire question. Many people seemed to see in the words of no.129 of the 'Ecumenical Directory' a breaching of the wall, a genuine way forward. Some at least suspect that the whole reason for 'One Bread One Body' was a plugging of this perceived gap: after all, it is virtually unknown for the Conferences of Bishops of these islands to do anything together. They have not even been able to come to a common mind with regard to posture at the celebration of Mass, and all of a sudden they appeared with this 'teaching document' so that 'general norms on sacramental sharing' might be established in their territories. The suspicion must be that the motivating power came from 'on high'. The Foreword to 'One Bread One Body', signed by Hume, Brady, and Winning, is less than enlightening. On the one hand, it does say, "we look forward to the day when all obstacles to full visible communion are overcome, and all Christians can celebrate the Eucharist together, sharing as 'one body' the 'one bread' of the Lord". On the other hand, the 'general norms' which are set forth in the document seem to be more restrictive than they need to be, and indeed more restrictive than the 'Ecumenical Directory' itself. A cynic might suggest that the Directory had 'slipped through the net' on this one, and the bishops had been ordered to tighten the grip and plug the hole. It may just be possible that the reflective cynic, in this instance, is right. In a well thought-out, but also highly personal, article in 'The Tablet', Gerard W. Hughes SJ spelt out his unease with the whole project. He says this, among other things:

> "Although some phrases in 'One Bread One Body' sing to my soul, the overall sound is not of beautiful music but of cries of alarm and the screeching of brakes. The screeching is at its worst pitch in the latter part of the text, which presents norms for eucharistic sharing. The general ruling given is that Christians not in full communion with the Catholic Church may not receive the Eucharist at a Catholic Mass except if 'there is danger of death, or if there is some other grave and pressing need'."[14]

The 'Ecumenical Directory' begins with two basic principles:

Firstly, "eucharistic communion is inseparably linked to the full ecclesial communion and its visible expression".

Secondly, "the Catholic Church teaches that by baptism members of other Churches and ecclesial communities are brought into real, even if imperfect, communion with the Catholic Church". Here the reference is to 'Unitatis Redintegratio', no. 22. At Vatican II, it must be remembered, there was a lot of discussion on this, and it was finally accepted by a large number of bishops 'with a very bad grace'.

The conditions are spelled out wherein a member of another Church may ask for and receive the Sacraments of the Roman Catholic Church:

- In danger of death.
- In other circumstances of 'grave and pressing need' according to any procedures that may

142

have been agreed between the Roman Catholic church and the other Churches concerned.

- The person concerned cannot have recourse to a minister of his/her own church.
- The person must ask for the Sacraments on his/her own initiative.
- The person concerned must manifest the faith of the Roman Catholic Church in the Sacrament concerned (since it is not only the Eucharist which is at stake here, but also Penance or Anointing of the Sick).
- The person concerned must be properly disposed.

The obverse of this is put very succinctly:

"A Catholic who finds himself/herself in the circumstances mentioned above may ask for these Sacraments only from a minister in whose Church these Sacraments are valid or from one who is known to be validly ordained according to the Catholic teaching on ordination" (no.132).

Interestingly, where the Directory speaks of 'grave and pressing need', 'One Bread One Body' goes out of its way to inform its readers that "the Church's law requires the need to be both grave and pressing" (underlining in the text itself). Whatever might be made of making 'the Church's law' the supreme arbiter in these matters, there is a follow-up which is doubtless meant to be explanatory but ends up by becoming merely patronising: "Such a need is more than a passing desire, or something arising simply from the sadness of feeling left out of a particular celebration" (no. 108). The canonical nature of the whole treatment of the subject is overpowering: there is even a glorious 'Freudian Slip' where the paragraphs of the Ecumenical Directory are referred to as 'canons' (cf. footnote 204). And maybe this is the problem with the whole thing; it is about 'norms', rules, regulations, which have about them the whiff of an oppressive legalism which has built up its own system and frame of reference to the exclusion of all others – including that of sound theology, to say nothing of the Gospel. As Hughes says, there is here "an image of the Church which is legalistic, sterile, devoid of mystery, for it is quite clear in this text that anyone who is not a full member of the Catholic Church is normally barred from a Catholic Eucharist".[15] All of this merely goes to reinforce an impression which is abroad, not only outside the Roman Catholic Church but also within it that the Gospel is now being interpreted via the Code of Canon Law and the Catechism of the Catholic Church (not to mention a veritable multitude of documents emanating from the Roman Curia) – not the other way around, as it should be. Paul's injunction (ironically to the church in Rome) was : "Do not be conformed to this world" (Rm 12:2). The problem with the institutional church is that this is precisely what it has done; other churches and traditions can answer for themselves, but it is clear that the Church of Rome is still bewitched by secular forms of organisation and control.

Hughes makes the point – which can be readily verified by reference to the *Acta Synodalia* of Vatican II – that the bishops at the Council were originally presented with a document ('*Schema De Ecclesia*') on the nature of the Church. Central to its tone was a clarification of who was in the Church and who was out of the Church. The bishops, by the grace of God, rejected this schema and the much broader (and much more biblical and theological) '*Lumen Gentium*' (21.11.1964) was promulgated as a 'Dogmatic Constitution'. In fact, it is the foundational document of the whole of the 'theology of Vatican II'. 'One Bread One Body' seems to be reversing the trend and reverting to the pre-conciliar way of speaking of the Church; certainly, its vision has a much narrower focus than 'Lumen Gentium'.

> "There is an intimate connection between the Eucharist and the Church, but the Church is ultimately a mystery. Its membership cannot be measured by counting the baptism registers. This is not to deny the essential visibility of the Church. The vine is a scriptural image of the Church. Its branches and fruit are visible: its roots, on which the branches and fruit depend, are invisible" (The Tablet, 29.1.2000, p.79)

It is this dimension of 'mystery' that seems to be absent from 'One Bread One Body'. There has always been the suspicion that the close identification between the Church and the Sacraments which is inherent in all Roman Catholic theology of the latter can be carried too far, to the point where it almost looks as if the Church is dictating to God how His Grace is to be communicated and administered. This sense of ecclesiastical control goes well beyond the question of intercommunion. It arises in the matter of the non-admission to Communion of those who have been divorced and remarried; it shows itself in the almost hysterical insistence on 'individual confession' as 'the only ordinary means of reconciliation with God and with the Church' (Catechism of the Catholic Church, nos. 1484.1497); it shows itself in a very peculiar way with regard to the ordination of women – it is 'not possible' for women to be ordained.[16] The foundations for all of these attitudes – for that is what they are – are found in the documents of ecclesiastical authority itself. The impression is of a vast network of legislation and commentary which provides not only a system of 'precedents' but at some point takes on a life of its own and becomes an end in itself. In

145

such a context, appeal to the Gospel or other parts of the Bible is useless: their interpretation has already been decided and cannot be disputed. As time has gone on, the apparatus of all such documents has become more and more cumbersome; like a badly organised 'scholarly publication', they tend to have three lines of footnotes for every line of text; everything that is said has to be backed up by reference to ecumenical councils and the utterances of long-dead Roman Pontiffs. There is a strain in Roman Catholicism which tends to regard the Churches of the Reform as 'prisoners' of their adopted principle *'Sola Scriptura'* (and there is a sense in which many Churches have recognised that the principle is not enough by itself); the only problem being that the Roman Church itself has become a similar 'prisoner' – prisoner to what it considers Tradition. On analysis, what is proposed as 'Tradition' is, in fact, a series of traditions built up over the years which (in the interests of bolstering ecclesiastical authority, papal or otherwise) have been made to carry an authority they are not entitled to.

Without doubt, the time has come to break through this whole network of ecclesiastical documentation, and return to first principles and agreed sources. It is time 'to loosen up the log-jam on intercommunion'.[17] One way is to extend the range of 'exceptions' (so that the occasions on which the Eucharist may be shared become more numerous); that is hardly a true answer to the question, it is hardly satisfactory, and indeed does not make any real impact on the position of the Roman Catholic Church. An 'exception', after all, will never be anything other. Realistically, however, in many cases this might commend as all that can be achieved at the present time – but it would mean ignoring some of the 'letter' and all of the 'spirit' of 'One Bread One Body'.

However, there is perhaps another way to tackle the question, and that at a different level.

"The various churches will have to 'come clean' with regard to their faith in the Real Presence. There is not nor could there be any requirement to accept the doctrine of transubstantiation (a doctrine which is but rarely found in its pure form, even among Roman Catholics today); but there must be a measure of agreement as to what we are doing together at the Eucharist. The traditional Roman view is that of the 'higher' Eucharistic theology, in which the Eucharist is the summit towards which the search for Christian unity is tending. There is, however, another way: the Eucharist can also be thought of as the source from which the search for Christian Unity draws its strength and direction. The Vatican II image of '*Culmen et Fons*' can provide a useful model in this whole question. One thing is certain – something must be done quickly if the situation is not to degenerate into a free-for-all and good and committed people lose heart for want of encouragement."[18]

The idea of 'summit and source' appears in Vatican II's Constitution on the Liturgy ('*Sacrosanctum Concilium*' of 4.12.1963) no.10. The full text reads: "The Liturgy is the summit towards which the activity of the Church is directed; at the same time it is the fountain from which all her power flows. For the goal of apostolic works is that all who are made sons of God by faith and baptism should come together to praise God in the midst of His Church, to take part in her sacrifice, and to eat the Lord's Supper". See Abbot-Gallagher, 'The Documents of Vatican II', p.142. An important ingredient in any dialogue between the Churches of the Reform and the Roman Catholic Church has to be a consideration of the relation between the Gospel and the Church. The Reformed view is that, since Christ Himself is the host at the Table, means that the Church must not impose any obstacles: all who have received baptism and love the Lord Jesus Christ are invited to the Lord's Supper (WARC, Princeton Declaration of 1954). The Roman Catholic view, however, is that the celebration of the Eucharist is of itself a profession of faith in which the whole Church recognises and expresses itself; sharing the Eucharist, therefore, presupposes agreement with the faith of the Church which celebrates the Eucharist.[19]

Inevitably, all of this points in one direction – who do we think we are when we call ourselves a 'church'? B.E.M. (i.e. the Baptism, Eucharist, and Ministry document: Faith and Order Paper no.111, WCC Geneva 1982) shows great wisdom in referring back to the text of the First World Conference on Faith and Order (Lausanne 1927).

"In view of the place which the episcopate, the council of presbyters, and the congregation of the faithful respectively had in the constitution of the early Church, and the fact that episcopal, presbyteral and congregational systems are each today, and have been for centuries, accepted by great communions in Christendom, and the fact that episcopal, presbyteral, and congregational are each believed by many to be essential to the good order of the Church, we therefore recognise that these several elements must all, under conditions which require further study, have an appropriate place in the order of life of a reunited Church".[20]

Allowing for the somewhat 'structural' way Lausanne seems to view church unity (a vision which is not entirely without its adherents even today), there seems a clear line of thought. If we move away from such a 'structural' view of a reunited Church, might it not be possible for all of the three New Testament models so ably described by Lausanne to co-exist in one 'Great Church', a genuine *oikumene* or *katholike* (*ekklesia*)? With such a vision, ministries are mutually recognised (including the ministry of women) and the Sacraments are available to all. Is it too much to ask that the churches could begin to take seriously the concept of 'alongside-ness'?[21] After all, Christians are living in a world where they are placed 'alongside' others who either know nothing of their faith or would try to marginalise it. The pain felt by many thinking Christians at the present time is not that of being estranged from the world; they have a pretty clear idea that that somehow fits the New Testament insight. What they find more painful than all of that is their sense of alienation from one another as result of historicopolitico-ecclesiastical factors long forgotten.

These are only some of the ideas that Alastair and I used to 'bat around'; I caught up with his 'divine impatience'; I rather think that if I ever let it go, he would haunt me for the rest of my days. Occasionally, after thirty-odd years striving to bring differing viewpoints into some kind of contact with one another, there is a sense of overwhelming tiredness. When that happens, there are two things that keep coming into my mind:

-    the first is the great changes that I have witnessed in my lifetime: the throwing down of the Berlin Wall, a black African as President of South Africa, the dissolution of the Soviet Union, and (at a much more banal level) a Glasgow Rangers team taking the field in an Old Firm game with more Roman Catholics in it than the corresponding Celtic team. It does not do simply to accept things and imagine that 'that's the way it is' and nothing will ever change. This *has* to be the motivating force behind anyone's ecumenical effort.

- the second is the remembrance of the infectious enthusiasm of many people who seemed totally unfazed by the obstacles that are thrown in their path; I then see Alastair's slightly quizzical look, and I think, "OK, let's give it another whirl – you never know". After all, it was he who used to say – "Never forget the Holy Spirit".

Footnotes

[1] The One Bread, One Body of the title is *One Bread One Body. A Teaching Document on the Eucharist in the Life of the Church, and the Establishment of General Norms on Sacramental Sharing,* Catholic Bishops' Conferences of England and Wales, Ireland, Scotland (London-Dublin, 1998).

[2] Action of Churches Together in Scotland: Unity Faith and Order Commission: February 1994 – *Inter-communion: the Churches Agree and Disagree*, p.1

[3] The most important documents in this connection would be the following:
- Declaration of the Secretariat for Christian Unity *Dans Ces Derniers Temps* on the position of the Catholic Church regarding eucharistic sharing between Christians of different confessions (7.1.1970, AAS 62 (1970) pp.184-188)
- Instruction on Special Instances of Admitting Other Christians to Eucharistic Communion in the Catholic Church, Secretariat for Christian Unity, 1.6.1972: AAS 64 (1972) pp.518-525
- Communion of the Secretariat for Christian Unity *Dopo la Pubblicazione* of 17.10.73, on the interpretation of the Instruction of 1 June 1972 regarding Special Instances of Admitting Other Christians to Eucharist Communion in the Catholic Church: AAS 65 (1973) pp.616-619
- Directory for the Application of Principles and Norms on Ecumenism of the Pontifical Council for Promoting Christian Unity (olim the Secretariat for Christian Unity) of 25.3.1993; this was intended to supersede the previous *Ecumenical Directory*, published in two parts: Part I *Ad Totam Ecclesiam* on 14.5.1967, and Part II *Spiritus Domini* on 16.4.1970
- Both the Directory and *One Bread One Body* refer to the Code of Canon Law, can. 844,4; it specifies that Catholic ministers may give the Sacraments of Eucharist, Penance and Anointing of the Sick to other Christians not in full communion when in the judgement of the Ordinary (ie

the diocese bishop or other religious superior) there is a "grave necessity". The conditions are: such Christians must ask for these Sacraments of their own will, they must provide evidence of holding the Catholic faith regarding these Sacraments, and they must possess the required disposition. All of this is expressed in no.1401 of The Catechism of the Catholic Church of 11.10.1992 (ironically, the thirteenth anniversary of the solemn opening of Vatican II).

It is very difficult for Roman Catholics to distinguish the relative value and theological 'weight' of all these documents: a 'declaration' may be more than it seems; and 'instruction may be less directive than it sounds; as for a 'communication', it seems to be that it is just that. A 'directory' is something more substantial, though the 1993 version shows precious little evidence of being 'up to speed' on what had been happening since the publication of its predecessor. A 'catechism' is precisely that, "a statement of the Church's faith and of Catholic doctrine", "a sure norm for teaching the faith and thus a valid and legitimate instrument for Ecclesial communion" (John Paul II: Apostolic Constitution *Dispositum Fidei, prefaced to the Catechism, no 3:* The Doctrinal Value of the Text).

Documents such as *One Bread One Body* or the Reports of ARCIC or reports of the dialogue between the Roman Catholic Church and the World Alliance of Reformed Churches must take their place on the totem pole, even though they may be more insightful and forward-looking than anything that comes from the Vatican.

4 Directory for the Application of Principles and Norms on Ecumenism (Pontifical Council for Promoting Christian Unity) no.129

5 The Encyclical Letter *Et Unum Sint* of 25.5.1995 is a remarkable document, not only for what it says (by way of humble confession of historical – and historic – faults and restatement of the classic Roman "high papalism" of the nineteenth century) but also by what it invites its readers to pursue in dialogue. At one point (no.88) John Paul II admits that "the Catholic Church's conviction that in the ministry of the Bishop of Rome she has preserved, in fidelity to the Apostolic Tradition and the faith of the Fathers, the visible sign and guarantor of unity, constitutes a difficulty for most other Christians, whose memory is marked by certain painful recollections. To the extent we are responsible for these, I join my Predecessor Paul VI in asking forgiveness". But that is against the background of the earlier statement that "among all the Churches and Ecclesial Communities, the Catholic Church is conscious that she has preserved the

ministry of the Successor of the Apostle Peter, the Bishop of Rome, whom God established as her "perpetual and visible principle and foundation of unity". The reference is to Vatican II's Constitution on the Church *Lumen Gentium* (21.11.64), ch.III, no.23. The real thrust of the arguments comes in no. 97 of *Ut Unum Sint,* where John Paull II goes on to say: "The Catholic Church, both in her *praxis* and in her solemn documents, holds that the communion of the particular Churches with the Church of Rome, and of communion. Indeed full communion, of which the Eucharist is the highest sacramental manifestation, needs to be visibly expressed in a ministry in which all the Bishops recognise that they are united in Christ and all the faithful find confirmation for their faith". The Pope uses the question: "Do not many of those involved in ecumenism today feel a need for such ministry?" ie the 'ministry', of the Bishop of Rome. Empirical observation would suggest the answer is 'No'. It really is strange that the late Cardinal of Glasgow, Thomas J Winning, writing in *'The Scotsman'* on the occasion of John Paul II's 80th birthday should advance the thesis that the Pope "took the message of ecumenism and placed it in the heart of the Church" (*Scotsman*, 18.5.2000.p.14). Demonstrably, relations between the Roman Catholic Church and the Orthodox Church have never been worse: relations with the western churches of the Reform are 'on hold', and that is with as much of a positive 'spin' as can be found. Not surprisingly, the cardinal does not offer an argument, just a statement. *"Quod gratis asseritut, gratis negatur".* If there has been ecumenical advance in the pontificate of John Paul II, it has been in Jewish-Catholic relations.

[6] The only coherent up-to-date presentation of this aspect of traditional Roman theology is to be found in The Cathechism of the Catholic Church, nos. 1356-1372.

[7] The present *Liturgia Horarum*, vol. III, pp.524ff., has done its best to preserve the flavour of Aquinas' work, even though it is pressed into a slightly different mould from the pre-conciliar *Breviarium Romanum* (the edition to hand being the Marietti, Turin, edition of 1961). Where the Vatican II version scores is in its selection of biblical readings, and in the excerpt from Aquinas' *Opusculum 57, in Festo Corporis Christi.*

[8] It is worth recalling exactly what the Council of Trent said:

"Because Christ our Redeemer said that it was truly his body that He was offering under the species of bread, it has always been the conviction of the Church of God, and this Holy Council now declares again, that by the consecration of the bread and wine there takes place a change of the whole substance of the bread into the substance of the

Body of Christ our Lord and of the whole substance of the wine into the substance of His Blood. This change the holy Catholic Church has fittingly and properly called *transubstantiation*" (Session XIII, 11.10.1551, ch.4; cf. DS 1642).

There have been several attempts over the years to insist that the Roman Catholic Church's faith in the Eucharist cannot be expressed without using the language of 'transubstantiation'; the text of Trent is enough to show that that is pushing matters too far and falling into the trap of trying to explain what is, after all, the 'Mystery of Faith'.

[9] Cf. *A History of the Council of Trent* (London-Edinburgh 1957-1961, 2 vols); *Ecumenical Councils in the Catholic Church: an Historical Survey* (London-Edinburgh 1960); art, *Concile*, in Encyclopëdie de la Foi I (Paris 1965); *Conciliorum Oecumenicorum Decreta* (Freiburgh 1962). The dating of the writings is important and explains their influence on Vatican II (1962-1965).

[10] This has been abundantly clear since the publication of Hans Küng's doctoral thesis *Rechtfertigung. Die Lehre Karl Barths und eine Katholische Besinnung* (Einsiedeln 1957); ET *Justification* (London 1966); cf. also *The Council and Reunion* (London 1961).

[11] *Directory for the Application of Principles and Norms on Ecumenism* of the Pontifical Council for Promoting Christian Unity (25.3.1993). It should be kept in mind, however, that most Roman documents in the present pontificate have had to be examined by the Congregation for the Doctrine of the Faith (olim the Holy Office of Inquisition) and this may well explain the persistence of this outmoded (and often offensive) vocabulary. The tone is set right at the start (no. 2) where direct reference is made to the publication of the Code of Canon Law, the Code of Canons of the Eastern Churches, and the Catechism of the Catholic Church (1983.1990.1992 respectively); hence, the language of the Directory is not only stilted (and sometimes incomprehensible) but it is also forensic, legalistic and far from the tone required in a document which has such a purpose.

[12] *Unitatis Redintegratio* of Vatican II (21.11.64); *Orientalium Ecclesiarum* (of the same date) make it clear that the Eastern Churches are in a 'Special Position' in their relationship to the Roman Church.

> "Everybody also knows with what love the Eastern Christians enact the sacred liturgy, especially the celebration of the Eucharist .... Although these Churches are separated from us, they possess true sacraments, above all – by apostolic succession – the priesthood and the Eucharist, whereby they are still joined to us in a very close

relationship" (*UR*, ch. III, no.15)

> "Eastern Christians who are separated in good faith from the Catholic Church, if they ask of their own accord and have the right dispositions, may be granted the sacraments of Penance, the Eucharist and the Anointing of the Sick. Furthermore, Catholics may ask for these same sacraments from those non-Catholic ministers whose Churches possess valid sacraments..." (*OE*, no. 27).

Subsequent documents do not add anything substantial to this position taken by Vatican II. In passing, however, it might reasonably be asked how members of the great churches of the East enjoy seeing themselves described as "non-Catholic ministers". Interestingly enough, the 1993 Directory refers to the canons of the Eastern Churches but not Vatican II.

[13] Cf. Directory (1993) nos. 129-136

[14] Cf.Gerard W. Hughes: *Listen to the Music*, in *The Tablet* 22.1.2000, pp.78-9

[15] Cf. art. cit., p.79

[16] The Catechism of the Catholic Church (no.1577) offers this:

> "Only a baptised man (*vir*) validly receives sacred ordination: Code of Canon Law, canon 1024. The Lord Jesus chose men (*viri*) to form the college of the Twelve Apostles, and the Apostles did the same when they chose collaborators to succeed them in their ministry. The college of bishops, with whom the priests are united in the priesthood, makes the College of the Twelve an ever-present and ever-active reality until Christ's return. The Church recognises herself to be bound by this choice made by the Lord Himself. For this reason, the ordination of women is not possible."

For the record, the biblical sources quoted are: Mk. 3:14-19; Lk. 6:12-16; I Tim. 3:1-13; II Tim. 1:6; Tit. 1:5-9; then is added Clement of Rome Ad Cor. 42,4; 44,3; PG I, 292-293; 300. The "argument from the choice of the Lord" is not only a curious one, it is one that knows virtually no bounds. The Lord chose to live a life of poverty; the Lord chose to speak Aramaic; the Lord chose to be born of a Jewish family (and it is not the first time that that has been raised as a condition for 'true' Christianity); the Lord chose simple, unlettered persons as His first followers. The list could go on, but it is clear that the Church has not felt itself bound by any number of the Lord's choices. One thing is clear, however, the Lord did choose to reveal His Resurrection first of all to a woman, the 'apostle of the apostles', Mary of Magdala.

[17] John Fitzsimmons, *Growing Together: Thirty Years On*, in *For God's Sake ... Unity* (Wild Goose, Glasgow 1998), p.114

[18] Art. cit., pp.772-773. Among other things, it says this:

> "As day by day we prayed together and meditated on Scripture ... we realised afresh both the degree of spiritual communion we already share in the richness of our common liturgical heritage, but also the pain of our inability to share together fully in the Eucharist.... Sometimes those in interchurch families experience great pain, particularly in the area of eucharistic life ... Our vision of full and visible unity is of a eucharistic communion of Churches."

The Tablet's own leading article on the subject (p.743) adds this:

> "The *Mississauga* emphasis on 'degrees of communion' is a very positive one. The statement talks of 'fundamental communion of a common faith and a common baptism'. Of a 'rich and life-giving multi-faceted communion', and a 'communion of joint commitment to our common mission.' It is obviously no longer sufficient to talk starkly of Catholic and Anglicans being 'out of communion', a charge which has untold implications for access to the sacraments. At what point does sharing a common Eucharist become the effective sign of a communion already achieved rather than of a more perfect one still over the horizon?"

[19] Towards a Common Understanding of the Church. Reformed/Roman Catholic International Dialogue: Second Phase, 1984-1990. Geneva WARC 1991, p.55

[20] *Baptism, Eucharist and Ministry. Faith and Order Paper no.111*, WCC Geneva 1982, no.26, pp.25-26, and commentary p.26

[21] The phrase is borrowed from Harvey Cox, *The Secular City. Secularization and Urbanization in Theological Perspective*, New York-London 1965, p.273

Inter-Faith Dialogue, Religious Pluralism and the Lambeth Conference

Michael Ingham

An observation made almost ten years ago by Roman Catholic scholar Hans Küng has become something of an axiom today: *"There will be no world peace without peace between the world's religions. There will be no peace between the world's religions without dialogue between the world's religions."*[1]   In the emerging arena of inter-faith theology the remark has acquired the status of self-evident truth, and has both inspired and legitimised efforts among believers of differing faiths to pursue the goal of inter-faith dialogue, a goal that includes, but is not limited to, theological rapprochement.

Küng's comment was made in the course of his attempt to develop some theological groundwork for a Global Ethic. The Global Ethic is a statement by representatives of the major faith traditions setting out the basic moral principles on which all religions can agree as the basis for responsible global citizenship. It was adopted informally by a council of three hundred religious leaders at the Parliament of the World's Religions in Chicago in 1993 after being proclaimed at an outdoor ceremony to an attentive audience of ten thousand people. It was hoped it might one day acquire the status of a United Nations charter such as those on Human Rights and the Environment. Subsequent reflection and commentary have evolved the document into *A Call to Our Guiding Institutions* which became the central organising work of the 1999 gathering of the Parliament in South Africa.

The Global Ethic in its original and present forms represents an effort by world religions to address problems together. It has stimulated scholars, theologians and thoughtful believers all around the globe to think about the possibilities of inter-religious co-operation to relieve the hardships of our world and to face its challenges in a spirit of partnership rather than competition. This worthy ideal is not an easy task, of course, because we are not starting from scratch.

Religions have a long history of relationships with each other. Some of it has been hostile and violent. There are many victims of inter-religious strife on every continent, and wherever we live we are surrounded by people who bear the marks of suffering in their lives and in their communities at the hands of religion. Even well-intentioned and gentle practitioners of faith in many of the traditions have been taught that partnership with other believers, dialogue and co-operation with people of other faiths, is a betrayal of belief, a blasphemy against God.

Today there are urgent reasons to challenge these inherited suspicions and to find both a new spiritual vision to unite people across differing religious identities and a new theological determination to overcome these historic antipathies. We are aware, as no generation before us has been aware, of the fragile nature of life on this planet. We face enormous challenges in safeguarding humanity's future, in preserving environmental integrity, in ensuring equitable and sustainable development. We know this is a spiritual task and not simply a political task because it involves the way people believe, the way they live their lives, the way they see the very nature and purpose of human existence.

Robert Müller, former Assistant Secretary-General of the United Nations, writes:[2]

'Religions and spiritual traditions: the world needs you very much! You, more than anyone else, have experience, wisdom, insights and feeling for the miracle of life, of the earth and of the universe. After having been pushed aside in many fields of human endeavour, you must again be the lighthouse, the guides, the prophets and messengers of the ultimate mysteries of the universe and eternity. You must set up the mechanisms to agree, and you must give humanity the divine or cosmic rules for our behaviour on this planet.'

The comment, by a senior diplomat, is significant at least as an indication of the awareness in political and governmental circles that they alone are unable to effect substantial global change of the kind needed for planetary survival, and that religious and spiritual traditions are necessary partners in the endeavour. This challenge to religion, from an unusual direction,[3] presents the various traditions with an imperative to confront their own relationships, histories and theologies. There remains, of course, the question of whether the world is ready to receive cosmic rules determined by the world's religions. But the challenge to discern what they might be has been accepted.

Inter-faith gatherings typically draw together a wide assortment of believers, including those who tend to make members of the major religions a little uneasy, such as self-professed pagans and new-age enthusiasts. But within this cosmopolitan diversity there are powerful and common sentiments being expressed. All over the world children of every culture and belief are being traumatised by the threat of the future. There is a profound sense that neither enlightened governments nor market economies can provide the basis of hope human beings need to survive and to co-exist, but that religious and spiritual movements have the potential to do so. The inter-faith movement is becoming a focus for global spiritual aspirations towards a just and sustainable future.

The modern inter-faith movement is a hundred years old. Throughout the 20th century there was a growing interest among adherents of religion, and even among people who have abandoned any religion, in the possibility of harnessing the spiritual power of faith for global responsibility and peace. Even though people today are fully aware of the destructive potential of religion's darker side, many also know that faith has the capacity to change human lives, to transform individuals and societies for good. The migration of religions out of their geographic and cultural isolation, the mass movement of religious believers into all the major cities of the world, has brought a new cross-fertilisation of ideas and insights among traditions and new possibilities for mutual understanding. We now know that at the core of every religious tradition there is an ethical imperative toward justice, love and peace. Human beings are profoundly spiritual creatures who tend to give deep assent to beliefs which give life its highest meaning. It is, therefore, at the level of belief that religions can play a positive and unifying role. One of the most important questions of the new millennium will be, can humanity's beliefs be shaped toward global partnership rather than global hostility?

The 20th century saw some of the greatest advances in the history of inter-faith dialogue. It was a century of exploration in the building of bridges between global faiths which ought perhaps to be noted one of the great achievements of recent times. Religions have always been in contact with one another, of course, in local situations, but this is the first time we have seen the rise of global movements promoting consultations and co-operation among the world's religious peoples.

The 1998 Lambeth Conference in England, for example, featured for the first time Jews, Muslims, Hindus, Buddhists and Sikhs walking in procession with Christian leaders at the opening service in Canterbury Cathedral. It was a sign, by the Anglican Communion, of the desire for better relationships with other traditions by the Anglican Communion. The Conference itself had a full session on Christian-Muslim relations. Inter-faith issues were discussed by bishops in every section of the Conference. In his presidential address, the Archbishop of Canterbury said "I was delighted that representatives of other faiths were present at our opening service. There can be no doubting the importance of inter-faith dialogue and co-operation for the peace and well-being of the world."[4]

This Conference produced more on inter-faith relationships than any body in the Anglican Communion has every done, and I shall return to some of its work later. But we can see similar developments in other Christian world communions, and in other faith traditions as well. There seems to be an emerging awareness that religious competition and hostility are dangerous, a threat to the world's future, and that new bridges need to be built if the positive power of religion is to be harnessed in a constructive way.

There is a local imperative to this as well. Almost all of us now live and work alongside people of other living faiths. They are our neighbours and, in some cases, members of our family. In many places the rights of religious minorities are coming to be protected by law. In Western schools we have seen a change in religious education from, at one time, exclusively 'Christian propagation' now to 'multi-religious education.' Some school boards over the last few years have paused at a stage of 'no religious education' but this has proven in most places to be unsustainable. There is a growing acceptance throughout the Western world not only of the fact of religious plurality but the potential benefits of it.

These developments, however, elicit criticism and suspicion in traditional religious circles. Many religious faithful regard these things not as a sign of progress, but as a slide into confusion and fragmentation. There are countervailing forces at work in all the major religions, aimed at limiting the boundaries of inter-religious accommodation, at defining faith in such a way as to prevent any moderating or mitigating of its core doctrines. There are movements of protest, declarations and manifestos, prayer gatherings and political lobby groups all intent on opposing what is described as liberalism and unbelief, the fatal surrender of truth to the seductions of an emerging global consciousness.

One of the main sources of opposition to inter-faith co-operation comes from religious fundamentalism, which is on the rise all over the world in every major tradition. Fundamentalism is a reaction to intellectual and spiritual modernisation and to the rapid speed of change in modern societies. Karen Armstrong[5] has examined somewhat sympathetically the complex sources of fundamentalism in the three Western monotheistic religions, pointing out that modernity is often cruel to certain groups and that they tend to preserve their social identity by religious introversion. In times of large scale social dislocation, such as marks most societies today, fundamentalism can become a powerful political force. At its heart it constitutes a deep impulse to stem the tide of change that is sweeping away social and cultural traditions right across our globalised world. It tends to regard the inter-faith movement as a dimension of globalisation, and therefore inimical to cultural, social and religious identity.

Hardly anyone today underestimates the force or danger of religious fundamentalism. There is scarcely a more toxic combination than religion and fear. One of its characteristics, whether Christian or any other, is the capacity to galvanise and mobilise human emotions by the clever use of sacred text and proven tradition. Its power lies precisely in the ability to claim divine authorisation, the imprimatur of God, for ideas and developments it endorses and to offer people an intellectual and spiritual sanctuary from the threat of modernisation, real or perceived, through the enduring appeal of ancient and holy myths. Perceived as demonic, therefore, inter-faith gatherings are routinely picketed and protested by fundamentalist groups.

This is not the only difficulty. Mainstream conservatives – to be distinguished from fundamentalists – exhibit the same suspicion of the inter-faith movement. There is anxiety among religious conservatives that new relationships between religions will require the sacrifice of something foundational to faith, something that cannot be negotiated away without destroying belief itself. There is apprehension that the inter-faith movement is unconcerned with preserving religious identity, that it cannot be trusted to protected the irreducible core of faith which is at the heart of each religion. There is criticism that the erosion of traditional religious belief will actually undermine world peace, and that the best chance for survival is for the world's peoples to come together 'into one flock under one shepherd.'[6]

Both fundamentalism and mainstream conservatism see a common enemy in religious pluralism. Pluralism is an emerging school of thought in Western universities and seminaries which is trying to build theological bridges across which people of different faiths can travel. It wants to create a framework, a 'meta-theory', in which people can embrace each other in good conscience, without sacrificing their own religious identity, and without disparaging the identity of one another. It seeks to overcome both religious exclusivism, by which one tradition claims to posses all the truth to the denial of others, and exclusivism by which one tradition allows a measure of truth to others, but only insofar as they reflect the truth of that tradition itself. For pluralists, neither of these provides a very firm basis for dialogue or world peace.

Pluralism is a theological effort not to negate the differences between religions but to hold them together. It has a variety of leaders and champions, not all of whom agree with one another but, in general, all pluralists are searching for a way both to respect the distinctiveness, the uniqueness, of religions and at the same time to articulate their unity in the transcendent origin that lies beyond them. It is based on the conviction that simple tolerance and mutual respect are not enough, and that the faith traditions need to affirm each other within a larger theocentric framework. This leads inevitably to an investigation into the roots of the differing traditions, and a re-examination of the core revelation which gave rise to the community that responds to it and protects it. Hans Küng has said more recently that there can be no dialogue between religions without an examination of the foundation of each religion.

It is this re-examination of the foundation of faith that has the protectors of tradition deeply worried. They suspect that the real project of pluralism is to eradicate belief, to revise or eviscerate the central truth claims of faith in order to make it more possible to fit the religions together. Opponents such as the late Lesslie Newbigin warn that pluralism is nothing more than a modern Procrustes, lopping off those parts of religion which don't fit into the inter-faith bed. Disparate thinkers such as Newbigin, Gavin D'Costa, Alister McGrath and Cardinal Ratzinger have all warned that dialogue must not become more important than truth or doctrine.

It is important to acknowledge that there is a legitimate

concern here. Some enthusiasts in the inter-faith field and some theologians of the pluralist school, have not paid sufficient attention to the question of doctrinal integrity, to the authenticity of the Christian gospel in relationship to other faiths. McGrath, a conservative evangelical, complains that there is a tendency among pluralists to revive the Ebionite heresy, the idea that Jesus was simply a human figure, one of many outstanding religious figures but in the end only 'one of the boys.'[7] Obviously, he says, no genuine relationship between Christians and others can be bought at the price of abandoning faith in Jesus as the one in whom the full being of God came to dwell. In this McGrath is quite correct. Genuine pluralism in my view does not need to reject the divinity of Jesus Christ and would gain nothing by doing so.

The Roman Catholic church, in a recent document by the International Theological Commission[8], says dialogue with other religions can proceed only on the assumption that Christianity is the complete revelation of God to humanity, and that Jesus Christ is the only way to salvation for the whole of humankind. Other faiths are to be regarded as mere 'preparations for the Gospel' (preparatio evangelica). They are to be welcomed only insofar as they contain 'seeds of the Word' (spermatikoi logoi) which is Christ. This is the classic inclusivist position, the view that other people can be accorded a dim awareness of the light which is fully revealed only in the tradition we espouse. The Commission's position seems to mark quite a retreat from the spirit of the Second Vatican Council which spoke about the truth in other religions. The Commission says it is a 'clarification,' and warns believers that dialogue cannot be placed before the doctrinal coherence of Christianity.

These are useful warnings, although they are not in my view

fatal to religious pluralism nor to inter-faith dialogue. Pluralism holds that all the great religions of the world represent authentic pathways to God. It places God at the centre of the world's religions, not our own or any other tradition, and invites believers to see all the great religions as the work of God refracted through the culture and thought-forms of the world's different peoples. It does not deny God's self-revelation in Christ, nor in the Koran, nor in the Torah, nor in other sacred symbols. It proposes to hold them together, despite their obvious discrepancies, in the greater mystery of faith.

Pluralism appeals to those aspects of the modern Western mind which have long been suspicious of religion's potential to aggravate and divide, to claim truth for itself in an exclusivist way, and its tendency to deny other insights in science, social theory, humanities and the arts. Western consciousness is willing to grant a relative validity to religion as one way of viewing reality, but it is not prepared to grant ultimate validity to it, nor indeed to any other intellectual paradigm, and it is not sympathetic to inter-religious jealousies or struggles of supremacy.

This inherent disposition to pluralism, which is characteristic of post-modern secular Western culture, is now seen as a great danger by advocates of strict religious orthodoxy. Those who want to protect religion against the threat of accommodation or re-thinking of core doctrines have now turned their attention to a critique of the Western mind itself. The way has been paved for them by secular critics and non-religious writers,[9] as well as by most philosophers of the post-modernist schools who collectively question the intellectual assumptions of modernity as it has shaped Western culture[10].

In conservative religious institutions today there is a full scale intellectual assault on the foundations of modernity, on the values and assumptions of Western education. In particular there is an attempt to deconstruct the Enlightenment and to represent its achievements as a danger to the modern world. The Enlightenment is now routinely portrayed as a false and perilous venture into individualism and rationalism, without any apparent thought to the collective intellectual restrictions of the late Middle Ages, mostly imposed by various religious magisteria, to which it was itself a reaction. In fact, since the end of the Cold War the greatest opposition to Western culture in its current form is coming from religion itself – primarily from Islam outside the Western world and conservative Christianity within.[11]

So we see countervailing forces at work in today's religious scene. On the one hand we have renewed recognition of the potential of religions to enhance and promote the well-being of humanity. The inter-faith movement is a growing phenomenon and is no longer an eccentric fringe on the edge of the major religions. All over the world theologians and ordinary believers are searching for ways of moving beyond mere tolerance, which is a precariously shifting ground, to the more solid foundation of a common vision among faiths and a common ethic propelling religions to move from hostility to partnership.

On the other hand we see a concern to preserve the integrity of belief against relativism or the trading away of cherished truth in pursuit of false compromise. In the face of the catastrophic decline of all the major religions in the West, there is a strong desire among many believers to resist theological developments which might cut the nerve of mission or evangelism. The task for many believers in the West today is to ensure their own survival. This makes for very focused doctrinal priorities and for a deep suspicion of competing communities of belief.

167

I want to argue that there is something of value in both these polarities. Although they seem to be opposed, they are in fact quite complementary and exhibit some common characteristics worthy of note. Both pluralism and orthodoxy share a concern for peace and justice. Orthodox believers are not intrinsically opposed to dialogue, indeed there have been dialogues between orthodox believers throughout the centuries, nor are pluralists necessarily opposed to the safeguarding of doctrine. What is at stake for them is the way doctrine is used, the way it is understood, the way its implications are presented for those who cannot hold to it. Still, despite all their opposing interests both have a conception of truth in which they deeply believe, a truth which is grounded inescapably in tradition itself.

Alan Jones, Dean of Grace Cathedral in San Francisco, writes:[12]

> "The fight is not between absolutists and relativists but between two views of the absolute... There are absolutes that cannot be grasped or put into words... our struggle with language will never end. We are pilgrims of the Absolute. Some people are protectors of the Absolute rather than pilgrims of it. God doesn't need looking after. The Absolute exists not as turf to be defended or as proof of one's own superiority, but as the horizon toward which one is for ever on pilgrimage."

Pilgrims and protectors each have valuable, though different, perspectives and usually need each other in the long run. Is there a way of affirming what is valuable and good in each of these approaches, in both pluralism and orthodoxy? Must they be necessarily opposed? The Anglican theological tradition (certainly of the sort embraced by Alastair Haggart) would, by instinct, resist the temptation to decide between them. Historically, Anglicanism has been reluctant to choose between conservation and progress in theology, unwilling to be seduced by definitions of orthodoxy which freeze Christianity into the past, or by a relativism which abandons Jesus Christ in order to accommodate other believers.

There may be some help for us here in the unusual story of American composer Charles Ives.[13] Ives had the rare capacity of being able to carry two tunes in his head at the same time. He could literally hear distinctly different compositions simultaneously without losing track of them. Apparently this developed when he was a child growing up in the small town of Dunbury, Connecticut. Each year on the 4th of July he would watch the parades processing down the main street. It was a rather short street, so the bands going down passed the bands coming up, each playing different tunes. Ives discovered he could recreate them afterwards exactly in his memory. (Ives could also play two tunes simultaneously on the organ, a talent for which he was fired from one Episcopal church!)

Can modern Christians learn to sing two religious tunes at the same time? Can we sing the song of the Christian tradition – the Nicene Creed, and the hymns, songs and poetry which proclaim Jesus Christ as redeemer of the world and saviour of all humanity – and can we at the same time sing the song of religious pluralism, which proclaims the saving activity of God in other ways, an infinite variety of ways, in this diverse and complex world? Can we sing the Lord's song as we have come to learn it, and a new song which places God at the heart of the universe, God at the centre of other ways of believing, God who is ultimately beyond our knowing and even perhaps beyond our religion? Are they in fact different songs?

One will be a Christocentric song, of course, the song centred in Jesus Christ as the final revelation of God for us. This is summed up in the liturgical creeds, which unite Christians of all traditions in the central and basic affirmations of the Church's faith[14]. The other will be a Theocentric song, which we will learn to sing with others who love, worship and obey God by a different name. This song is sung in the simple act of entering into spiritual relationships across religious boundaries. It is the implicit recognition that God is encountered in the tradition of the other, and that the symbols, language and culture of other traditions are vehicles of divine revelation comparable with our own.

It would be easy to object that this is intellectually dishonest, that these songs are disharmonious and incompatible, a blasphemy against Christ. But in fact we do sing different songs all the time. We couldn't live in the modern world unless we did. We sing ancient hymns written when people thought the earth was flat, and we translate them in our minds into the context of an expanding universe. We read sacred texts that presuppose ideas we no longer believe in, but we search those texts for eternal truths which still illumine and inspire us. We listen to language that excludes, according to the meaning of our age, but we try to hear it as including us, as inviting us in. We are modern technological people, computer nerds, scientists, or at least deeply influenced by the scientific world, and yet we dance in circles, we pray to the invisible depths, and we hold truths that are incapable of verification by anything except faith itself.

We are Canadians, or Americans, or British, and proudly so, and we are also global citizens. We sing two songs. We are men or women, yet we find we cannot build relationships without learning each other's wonderfully foreign music. We belong to political parties with deeply opposed convictions, radically different melodies, yet there is a larger idea called democracy to which we give our assent, and it requires that we grant others the right to sing their different melody from time to time.

Can Christians learn to sing with Jews, Muslims, Buddhists, Sikhs and members of other faiths without either surrendering our Christian voice or trying to take over the whole choir? All Christians today, of whatever variety, in fact have developed the Ivesean capacity to hold different tunes together. The urgency of the global situation, however, now requires the development of that capacity in an inter-faith direction. Like any new music, the mastery of it will require a change of attitude and a willingness to go to choir practice. Anglicans at least have been encouraged to do this by the recent statements of the Lambeth Conference, to whose advances in inter-faith dialogue I now turn.

The documents of the 1998 Conference[15] contain *Thirty Theses on Inter-Faith Relations.* These are remarkable statements, unfortunately buried in the dense text of the Section 2 Report. They deserve special attention, perhaps even separate publication, because most Anglicans and, it seems, many bishops are unaware of their adoption by the Conference.

These thirty short declarations represent a significant advance over earlier positions of Lambeth Conferences, whose statements on inter-religious matters in a period of just over a hundred years reveal a gradual but unmistakeable shift towards greater inter-religious openness and away from theological exclusivism. Indeed, they are a remarkable set of affirmations by a Christian world Communion and offer much hope for improved inter-faith relationship if they can be put into practice at the grassroots level.

I reproduce them here to draw attention to their theological and practical importance for global dialogue. Many of them may seem simple or obvious, but one should bear in mind the substantial fact of their being formally affirmed by a worldwide Christian body.

Thirty Theses on Inter-Faith Relations

1.   We must have a real desire to listen to people whose faith and world-view are different from ours.

2.   Respect for the faith of others should not allow us to mock the beliefs and practices of others.

3.   We should be determined to believe the best about others.

4.   We will want to recognise gladly all the common ground that we can find, and at the same time all the differences.

5.   There needs to be a spirit of repentance which arises out of an awareness of the genuine wrongs and even crimes that Christians have committed in the past.

6.   We need to recover the right kind of confidence in the message of the Gospel. By this is meant "a humble recognition that there is something distinctive about the message concerning Jesus for people of all faiths, and it will spring at its best from a spontaneous desire to share what we know of Jesus Christ."

172

7.   Christians need to work as far as possible for genuinely open and loving human relationships with people of other faiths.

8.   Generalisation based on one situation cannot easily be applied to another, since political and social contexts vary so much from one part of the world to another.

9.   Christians need to be willing and able to talk about anything that is of interest and concern to people of other faiths.

10.   Even in situations where dialogue seems impossible, there should be a real desire for face-to-face meeting, frank exchange of opinion and peace-making.

11.   The way religious communities relate to each other in one part of the world can have immediate and far-reaching effects on communities in other parts of the world.

12.   In the context of genuine relationships, it is entirely natural for Christians to share their deepest convictions.

13.   The content of the Christian message is likely to focus on the person of Christ.

14.   Our approaches to people of other faiths are likely to be influenced profoundly by our understanding of salvation.

15.   Christians need to know more about other faiths and to develop an understanding of them.

16.   Christians will want to seek the total well-being of others.

17. Christians should be willing to work as far as possible in co-operation with people of other faiths in addressing human concerns and working for justice, human rights and the environment.

18. In situations where there is persecution, Christians should adopt special attitudes of patience and perseverance.

19. Christians must be prepared to engage in advocacy on behalf of fellow Christians in difficult situations.

20. Churches in situations where these difficulties do not exist have a special obligation to support suffering churches in other parts of the world.

21. Many of the most difficult issues in inter-faith relations today are caused by the rise of fundamentalisms of different kinds.

22. Christians must be able and willing to present the Gospel in ways that are culturally appropriate.

23. We cannot avoid the difficulties associated with people of other faiths becoming disciples of Christ and accepting baptism.

24. There are situations where clear pastoral guidance is needed by Christian congregations.

25. Christians can and should appeal to the principle of reciprocity. This means we need to advocate for the rights of religious minorities in our own context just as we would expect the same rights for Christians where they are a minority.

26. Christians want to make Christ known and give others the opportunity of following him. They are not however seeking to convert or in the business of conversion in the sense that their sole aim is to make the other person change his or her beliefs.

27. The word 'proselytising' refers to making converts by methods that are not appropriate, such as bullying, manipulation, use of material resources, targeting specific persons or groups for conversion, misusing power or privilege, or seeking to make Christians who are carbon copies of ourselves.

28. An ecumenical approach is needed in developing our responses to people of other faiths.

29. We need to find the most appropriate structures to facilitate the sharing of news, information, ideas and resources relating to inter-faith concerns.

30. In addition to the kind of sharing we propose, there may be a need to find ways of developing specific strategies throughout the Communion.

A more extended commentary on these declarations than I can offer here is needed for Anglicans and other Christians working in the field of inter-faith dialogue and theology. They require, perhaps, a full exegesis (certainly one of greater generosity than accompanies them in the Final Report itself). We can note here, however, some of the more significant of the theses, in particular those which challenge conventional assumptions in the church about our attitudes and responsibilities to people of other faith traditions.

They begin by addressing the way we think of other believers, stressing the importance of intellectual and spiritual openness, an attitude of respect, and the desire to listen. While this may seem unremarkable, it need hardly be said that such qualities have been absent in many places and times from Christian minds and hearts, with disastrous consequences. The bishops recognised that the quest for peace and mutual understanding cannot begin from a position of contempt. The polemical misrepresentation of other ways of believing for evangelistic or missionary purposes is here rejected.

Reference to the need for repentance for the crimes Christians have done in times of missionary zeal is also highly significant. Churches do not repent easily, if at all, despite their exhortations to the faithful to do so themselves. Pope John Paul's public prayer earlier this year seeking forgiveness for the church's treatment of women, aboriginal peoples, and people of other faiths is a demonstration of the next step such declarations require, namely liturgical enactment. Implicit in this call to repentance is an imperative to reconsider not only our actions with respect to other traditions, but our theology as well. Missionary practice flows from prior theological precepts. Küng's call to a reconsideration of the theological foundations of each religion finds an echo here, and although that work is well under way in some seminaries and universities it is also strongly resisted by the guardians (and fundraisers) of traditional missionary polity.

Such a reconsidered missiology is not an abandonment of the missionary enterprise nor cowardice in the face of hostility. The Conference affirmed the need for 'the right kind of confidence in the message of the Gospel' (thesis 6). This confidence is based on the distinctiveness of God's revelation to the world in Jesus Christ, a revelation Christians believe is to be shared humbly with others in the conviction that we have something both to teach and to learn. Central to the Gospel is the person and work of Jesus Christ, who will remain for Christians the primary impetus in the search for mutual respect and global justice.[16]

There is much attention in the theses to the political and social realities of inter-faith hostility. Many of the bishops present at Lambeth live and work as members of a religious minority facing daily harassment and persecution. It is noteworthy that this fact did not persuade them to adopt a merely reactionary position, as it was tempting to do. The declarations urge face to face meetings between religious leaders in situations of tensions, eschew the desire to demonise or bear false witness against others even in the face of similar provocation, and in those circumstances where dialogue is impossible they counsel patience and forbearance so as not to bring Christ into disrepute or cause the situation to deteriorate.

The 'principle of reciprocity' (thesis 25) is of special significance. The obligation of Christians to advocate for the rights of religious minorities in Christian societies is the ethical consequence of our equal obligation to support persecuted churches. This moral principle cuts against much contemporary practice, where many are more publicly vocal on one side of the equation than the other. The application of this principle in Western societies (for example, to the much publicised 'prayer in schools' debate in North America, as well as other similarly controversial political and social questions) demands further elaboration. For a Christian world communion to articulate the principle formally, however, is a remarkable thing, and the active prosecution of the principle by Christian churches throughout the world would go a long way toward reducing tensions in some religious contexts.

These Lambeth theses are helpful theologically not least because they clarify several terms frequently misused in current discussions, distinguishing the separate meanings of words that are frequently lumped together indiscriminately in popular discussion. Evangelism, conversion, and proselytism are commonly used in unhelpful ways that cloud better understanding of the church's proper mission. Lambeth '98 offered some clarifications which would bear wide dissemination.

Evangelism was distinguished from both proselytism and conversion. Thesis 26 affirms that Christians want to make Christ known and give others the opportunity of following him. But 'Christians are not seeking to convert or in the business of conversion in the sense that their sole aim is to make the other person change his or her beliefs.' This makes it clear that conversion is God's business, not the church's, and implicitly recognises that it happens both away from, and in the direction of Christianity. Lambeth thereby distanced itself from much that is done today in the name of evangelistic outreach.

Much current writing on evangelism separates into two fundamentally different schools of thought. One - generally arising from the Western church growth movement - sees it in terms of turning other believers into Christians and (not incidentally) extending the global power and influence of the church. This view is often accompanied by theologies of Christian exclusivism which hold that only Christians can be saved and that the Kingdom of God will arrive by converting the world to faith in Jesus. The other arises both from the reflections of Christians living as religious minorities in non-Western countries and from the global inter-faith movement. This sees evangelism primarily as 'witnessing to Christ' through diaconal acts of service and mercy to others, and through joyful unapologetic preaching of Christ but without the hidden agenda of conversion. Here, tolerance and mutual respect go together with freedom to practise and teach one's beliefs.

Evangelism was also distinguished from proselytism. "Proselytising refers to making converts by methods that are not appropriate, such as bullying, manipulation, use of material resources, targeting specific persons or groups for conversion, misusing power or privilege, or seeking to make Christians who are carbon copies of ourselves" (thesis 27). The exploitation of poverty of weakness by Christian (or any other) agencies to 'win souls' was thus declared unacceptable. So was the targeting of Jews, Muslims or any other group. The principle of reciprocity would mean the rejection of proselytism among Christians by people of other faiths too.

The distinction between evangelism as 'conversion' and as 'witnessing' is crucial. Lambeth supported the second, and it would follow that if Christians want to do this kind of evangelism ourselves, we must allow the same freedom to others. Such tolerance of co-existence, and even friendly competition, among religions is observed more in the breach than in the adherence in many parts of the world. As a step towards global stability it will require a great leap of faith for many Christians.

These thirty theses cannot be construed as a product of the religious pluralist school. They are quite conservative and cautious in many respects, and would not go far enough to satisfy those who, with English theologian John Hick, have 'crossed the Rubicon' from a Christocentric to a Theocentric world view. They are, nevertheless, a step away from the historic exclusivism of our tradition and a step towards the kind of theological re-visioning called for by Küng and others.

179

Religious pluralists argue for a future where believers can witness their faith to each other without needing to become the dominant voice. They believe such a world would be better than this one, and that religious competition is in any case unnecessary because God has made himself known in many ways. In a pluralistic world, they argue, it makes no more sense to pity other believers because they are not Christians than to pity other Christians because they are not Anglicans. This is not to surrender Jesus Christ to some sort of intellectual relativism. It is rather to see that commitment to Jesus Christ today requires a search for truth in each religion. These theses are not especially radical, but they do represent a way of singing two songs in the strange land where God has placed us. They are a call for dialogue, for mutual respect, and they go beyond mere tolerance which is so often simply a strategy of power. They are not a betrayal of Christ, or of Christian convictions about Christ, but rather, in a spirit of obedience to the universal Logos which became incarnate in him, they invite Christians to see the grace of God beyond the Christian religion and to acknowledge God's redemptive activity in the deep faithfulness of other people. They support the missionary work of the church but not at the expense of inter-faith relationships. They encourage evangelism, but in such a way as to respect the same rights of others to promote and advance their own distinctive beliefs.

There are many obstacles to religious peace and co-operation, but here at least is some hope and encouragement. As worldwide Christianity struggles with the debilitating effects of globalisation, environmental and economic exploitation, and the internal conflicts that afflict every religion, here are some signs of what I have called 'grounded openness'[17] – that is, a deep commitment to Christ which opens people up to the fresh discovery of God in other places. The current culture wars in the church are a sinful distraction from our more pressing tasks. We need to find that deeper unity that enfolds us. To do that we must learn to embrace that essential requirement of harmony, namely plurality, and nowhere more so than in its religious dimensions.

Footnotes

[1] See Global Responsibility: In Search Of a New World Ethic, Hans Küng, New York: Crossroads, 1991

[2] Quoted in *A Source Book For the Community of Religions,* Joel D Beversluis,   ed, Chicago: Council For The Parliament Of The World's Religions, 1993

[3] There have been many others too, especially from the scientific and environmentalist communities. See *Global 2000 Revisited*, Gerald O Barney, ed. Chicago: The Millennium Institute, 1993

[4] See *The Lambeth Conference (1998): Final Report,* London: Anglican Consultative Council, 1999

[5] See *The Battle For God,* New York: Alfred, A Knopf, 2000

[6] There are many advocates of alarm. One of the most influential is Bishop Lesslie Newbigin in *The Gospel In A Pluralist Society,* London: SPCK, 1989. See also *Christian Uniqueness Reconsidered: The Myth Of A Pluralistic Theology of Religions,* Gavin d'Costa, ed. Maryknoll: Orbis Books, 1998

[7] See "Jesus The Only Way? Anglicanism And Religious Pluralism" in *The Truth About Jesus,* Donald Armstrong, ed. Grand Rapids, Michigan: William B Erdmann's 1998

[8] *Christianity and the World Religions*, International Theological Commission, Vatican Documents, 1997

[9] For example, Allan Bloom in *The Closing Of The American Mind, London, Simon & Schuster, 1998; and also John Ralston Saul's Voltaire's Bastards: The Dictatorship Of Reason In The West,* Viking Books 1992 – a brilliant evisceration of rationalism and its misuses in the modern Western era.

[10] See, for example, Michael J Scanlon's "The Postmodern Debate" *in The Twentieth Century: A Theological Overview, Gregory Baum, ed. Maryknoll: Orbis Books, 1999*

[11] See *Fundamentalism in Comparative Perspective,* Lawrence Kaplan, ed. University of Massachusetts Press, 1992

[12] Quoted in Bishop William Swing's *The Coming United Religions,* Grand Rapids, Michigan: Co-Nexus Press, 1998. The United Religions Initiative, founded by the Episcopal bishop of San Francisco, is one of the fastest growing global inter-faith organisations.

[13] As told in *Liberal Evangelism: A Flexible Response To The Decade*, by John Saxbee, Bishop of Ludlow, SPCK, 1994

[14] The Nicene Creed significantly contains no comment on other religions and is not a theologically exclusivist document. The phrase "for us and for our salvation he came down from heaven" is read by religious pluralists as referring to Christians and not to members of other religious faiths.

[15] See note 4.

[16] It is interesting to note that the theses refer to the "distinctiveness" of Christ in the world's religions, perhaps indicating by a nuance the difficulty of speaking of the uniqueness of Christ" which has become code language in conservative circles for theological exclusivity.

[17] See *my Mansions Of The Spirit: The Gospel In a Multi-Faith World*, Toronto: Anglican Book Centre, 1997

Beyond political correctness

David Haslam

The origins of the term 'political correctness' lie somewhere within the political right of the United States. It is a term which appears to have been coined in order to undermine progressive initiatives in the fields of race, gender, sexuality and disability. A recent report from a 'Racial Consultants' Day' of the United Reformed Church went so far as to describe political correctness as 'a term people use to dismiss the behaviour and language of justice'. Indeed certain newspapers and political commentators seem to take great delight in pronouncing initiatives towards equality as 'politically correct', thereby implying they are some kind of peculiarity dreamed up by modern equivalents of the 'loony lefties' of the sixties and seventies. By definition, they imply, something described as 'politically correct' need not be taken seriously.

It is a clever and confusing term, because there is a grain of truth in its criticisms. It is clever because, while accepting in all apparent seriousness that there is a problem in certain areas of our society, those using it demolish every suggestion to actually *do* something by trotting out the 'politically correct' label. A classic recent example has been the Inquiry into the death of Stephen Lawrence, where Judge MacPherson and his colleagues, having spent an enormous amount of time and public money, made some seventy recommendations. The right-wing press, while beating their breasts about the police errors, vigorously attacked not only most of the recommendations but the Inquiry Report itself. Even before it was published, the *Daily Telegraph* stated in an editorial that political correctness is a greater problem for the police than racism. It pontificated, 'The number of people who have actually experienced police racism is almost certainly smaller than the number who have suffered from crimes while local policemen (sic) were attending racism awareness courses'.[1]

The term confuses because there can indeed be an element in some supposedly progressive initiatives which is shallow, false or simply window-dressing. Some years ago one English local authority elected its first black mayor, with much fanfare. Unfortunately the person concerned was really not up to the job. The 'mayor's gaffes' were gleefully reported by those who pointed to political correctness as the reason for his election and were happy to mock the black community. We need to unpack the idea of 'political correctness' and look at it in a little more depth, to disentangle the grains of truth from the mischief-making.

The intention of those accused of political correctness may well be to do the right thing, but they need to understand that there are at least three dimensions to what they might be aiming for. The first is that of '**superficial correctness**', when an initiative is being undertaken to deflect criticism, without proper understanding of the problem it seeks to address. Superficiality leads to tokenism, where an action is taken or someone installed in a particular position as a genuine but naive gesture in the direction of equality, such as the mayor mentioned above. The intention is, wittingly or not, that the wider institutional realities do not have to change. Such actions give rather easy grounds for the jibe of 'political correctness'.

Examples of superficiality are lampooned by the tabloid press with great glee. However in many cases they turn out to have been incorrectly reported, and to contain at least an element of the next and more important dimension, which might be described as '**justicial correctness**'. This is a term to send a shudder down the spine of linguistic purists - Alastair Haggart would certainly have expressed distaste - but I cannot find another phrase which is both simple and descriptive. What I mean by it is that an initiative exhibiting this quality really will lead to a fairer situation, and those who are disadvantaged in the current context will be better and more fairly represented as a result.

The final dimension of the reality behind the term, particularly perhaps for Christians or those of religious belief, is that of **theological correctness**. By this I mean that something is right and proper in the light of the teaching of Christianity or indeed of most faith communities. There may of course be some overlap between what is justicially correct and what is theologically correct, but it is important for Christians to be able to undergird theologically initiatives they believe to be based on justice. The different dimensions may be illustrated in the 'equal opportunities' debate. For a body to adopt 'equal opportunity policies' is superficial correctness, unless such policies make a difference. To achieve justicial correctness there needs to be equality of outcome, i.e. the results need to be measured. Theological correctness involves a belief that each human being is of equal worth and therefore entitled to an equal share, not only of the opportunities of our society, but also its resources.

Taking the debate forward

Let us look at three areas in which the accusation of political correctness is often levelled and see where there might be merely superficiality, and what justicial and theological correctness might demand. These are language, employment and the work of the police. **Language** can be something of a battlefield in this whole field and I have written elsewhere about what I call 'colour-coded language'[2]. The lunatic fringe in this debate can be found among those tabloids who carry stories such as school-children being banned from singing 'Baa-baa black sheep'. Apart from the fact that that particular story turned out to have little factual basis, there is a more serious issue in the constant use of the adjective 'black' to convey a negative message. Examples are black spot, day, economy, mail and indeed sheep. We will come back to the latter shortly.

We then have the adjective 'black' used in purely descriptive terms, such as blackout, black eye, black coffee and so on. This is where the lunatic fringe comes in again, using the 'political correctness' sneer to suggest that one should ask for coffee 'without milk', rather than 'black'. The whole debate then becomes devalued. The song 'Baa, baa black sheep' is interesting because *apparently,* in the song, 'black' is not used in a pejorative way, but at the same time the phrase 'black sheep', usually of a family, *is* a pejorative term and caution therefore needs to be exercised in its use, even in a children's song. Those who try to belittle the effect of language should read the poem entitled *What shall I tell my Children?,* by a young black mother furious about bringing up a black child in a world where things labelled 'black' are often bad, those called 'white' almost always good.

Language expresses our attitudes and thought-forms, and needs to be carefully monitored. If colour-coded language is oppressive to a minority, on grounds of justicial incorrectness it should not be used. If such language belittles in any way a child of God, *even if it is only in their perception*, it is theologically incorrect, even sinful, and should be avoided.

[This takes us into the wider debate about terminology. One aspect of this is the use and meaning of the word 'race'. If there is only one race, the human race, how can we ever talk about 'races' or even 'racial groups'? We can however speak of 'racism' because that describes an ideology which believes that there *are* different races and that some of these are inferior. We can also speak legitimately of 'institutional racism' which enshrines that ideology - sometimes unthinkingly - in an institution's norms and practices. I have defined institutional racism as 'the effects of a combination of historical inequalities and an ideology of racial superiority - either overt or covert - which between them result in particular ethnic groups being discriminated against both in the opportunities offered and the sanctions operated within a given society'[3]. The Macpherson report says it consists of 'the collective failure of an organisation to provide an appropriate and professional service to people because of their colour, culture or ethnic origin. It can be seen or detected in processes, attitudes or behaviour which amounts to discrimination through unwitting prejudice, ignorance, thoughtlessness and racist stereotyping which disadvantage minority ethnic people'. 'Unwitting' is a key word here which needs to be remembered.

Both these definitions omit the concept of power, and how crucial it is that those with power, within organisations or outside, address the situation. They also beg the question of the use of the adjectives 'racial' or 'racist'. The latter is generally appropriate, coming directly from the noun 'racism'. The former we may need to think more about. At present it often describes behaviour arising out of racism, e.g., racial attacks, racial superiority, racial prejudice. However 'racial discrimination' should perhaps more accurately become 'racist discrimination', and the term 'racial equality' may become more suspect as, while pointing towards positive changes, it implies there actually are separate races which need to be treated equally. It may need to be replaced by 'ethnic equality'.

Finally, how best do we describe the communities to which we refer. 'Black' is perhaps being used less, although it remains the strongest political statement for many. 'Ethnic' is increasingly employed as an adjective - we need to remember we are all 'ethnic' - 'minority ethnic communities' or 'black and minority ethnic communities' seem the best overall descriptive phrases to use. The latter could be criticised on length as well as political correctness, but if it is justicially and theologically correct then we will have to live with the criticism. It is rather like replacing the term 'Third World' with 'the people of Asia, Africa and Latin America' (and the Caribbean?). It may take longer to say or write, but if it is how people wish themselves to be described it should be done.

The second area to explore is that of **employment**, where superficial correctness in terms of tokenistic appointments can sometimes occur. In the sixties and seventies it became useful in marketing terms for companies in the United States to have one or two high profile minority managers, directors or other spokespersons. The same was true of Government. The more astute representatives of minority communities soon began to point out that this apparent change of heart was tokenistic, superficial, even less than skin deep. It did not appear to be making any difference to the lower echelons of these organisations, or the distribution of their resources.

Hence a push for 'affirmative action' programmes began to develop. These required changes in the recruitment and selection of the workforce, training for selectors and managers, and regular monitoring of the results. These changes soon began to be attacked by those attacking 'political correctness' as 'positive discrimination', bringing in people simply because of their colour or minority status without reference to their ability. The grain of truth in their argument appears again here, because sometimes this was a factor. It

188

is not however helpful to select and promote people simply because of their colour or ethnic origin. If they are not up to the position this will cause a backlash and set back the whole process of change.

Part of the debate in the employment field has taken place around the term 'equal opportunities'. If the chances are equal, the argument goes, it is fair for all. Here, to see what would be justicially and indeed theologically correct we need to bring in the concept of the 'level playing field'. If the field is not level for minorities, then all the equal opportunities policies in the world will make no real difference. This in fact is what appeared to be happening in the eighties and nineties in the U.K. What was then the Community and Race Relations Unit of the Council of Churches, later to become the Churches Commission for Racial Justice, undertook a survey in 1989 of the 100 top employers in the U.K. A reply rate of 25% was achieved. What became clear was that although many large employers had equal opportunities policies, there was not much training attached, little monitoring of results and minimal change in the actual employee profile.

The principles under which good affirmative or positive action programmes operate are that there must be clearly expressed policies, training for staff involved in implementing them, monitoring of the results and a key person at the top of the organisation - preferably in a company the Chief Executive - who ensures that progress is being made. Out of the above survey the C.C.R.J. helped to develop the *Wood-Sheppard Principles for Race Equality in Employment*,[4] a set of ten principles which any employer could follow to lay the foundation for a scheme of positive action to level the playing-field. It was envisaged that this would help the Churches themselves to become better employers and give them a tool to offer companies in which they were investing, to do the same.

Although affirmative action policies are being pushed back to some degree in the United States, by those screaming 'political correctness', they have produced a situation where at least some major companies produce an annual 'employee profile', which sets out in a one-page table the number of minority (and women) workers in the company and at what grade they are employed. It is therefore possible to see, year on year, whether there are changes and whether the workforce both in numbers and in seniority, is more-or-less reflective of the community from which it draws its personnel. Some British companies, especially banks, building societies and retailers, are beginning to move in the same direction. In this field positive action has shown itself to be the justicially and theologically correct approach. It may be added that the same principles are applicable to voluntary organisations and posts, and this is particularly important for institutions such as the Churches. In relation to the police service, there were many debates in the aftermath of the Stephen Lawrence Inquiry, and several policy initiatives from the police, even before the Inquiry had reported. Some of these have been greeted with scepticism by black and minority community representatives, including the Black Police Association (B.P.A.). The B.P.A. came into their own during the Inquiry and were able to give the lie to the 'correctness' lobby's message that this was just a tragic aberration, that there were a few bad apples in the barrel, but if you got rid of them all would be well. The B.P.A. insisted there was an endemic institutional problem in the Metropolitan Police Service, as in all police forces, and there needed to be fundamental change. This was backed up by research from academics such as Robin Oakley and Simon Holdaway, the latter writing not about the 'canteen culture' but the deeper occupational culture of the police. He argued that racism, as well as sexism and other problems, were so deep within the collective psyche of the police service that they had to be addressed at a fundamental level. The Home Office response to the Lawrence Inquiry is still emerging as this essay is being written. Targets for black and minority officers have been set for all of the 40-plus police authorities in England and Wales. This means they will need to retain minority officers as well as recruiting them, retention having proved difficult in the past because of the attitudes such officers have encountered. Training has been intensified. Racial harassment units have been set up. The 'Met.' has been inspected. The police are to come under the Race Relations Act. Advertising campaigns have become more minority-friendly, more vigorous. Only time will tell whether the reforms have gone far or deep enough. Meanwhile the reaction from quarters such as the *Daily Telegraph* or the *Daily Mail* is as suggested above, that 'political correctness' is the problem rather than police racism. The fact is that almost all the reforms suggested by the Lawrence Inquiry can be described as justicially correct, aiming to change both attitudes and practices to reflect real equality. And if attitudes cannot always be changed then practices must be, so that stereotyping and prejudice cannot hold sway.

Theological correctness requires that those in the Churches must constantly admit, when in dialogue with other institutions and employers, such as the police and major companies, that we are also sinners and that we have not yet got it right. This has come to me afresh during the autumn of 1999 when, as a member of the Anglican Bishop of Southwark's Inquiry into Racism in the Diocese, I heard a range of black and minority people from the diocese express vigorously their views on the institutional racism - quite often unwitting - hidden in the structures and practices of the Diocese. This resulted among other things in minorities being seriously under-represented in decision-making at diocesan, deanery and local parish level. The fact that the Churches were also wrestling with the problem was always communicated to police spokespersons when the C.C.R.J. met with them, sometimes by Bishop Alastair himself. Repentance may be derided as politically correct, but it is nevertheless a theologically correct prerequisite for continuing progress towards racial and ethnic equality.

What is to be Done?

We need to operate on at least three levels, personal, church and society. In the first of these the struggle is ongoing. Moving to south London in late 1998 I went into a local doctor's surgery to register. Behind the counter were two older white women and a young black woman, discussing the files. The receptionists, I thought, they will soon send me in to see the doctor. Two of the women went out and a little later the remaining (white) receptionist said to me, 'Your doctor is in the room at the end on the left'. When I entered the room, seated at the desk was the young black woman I had assumed must be a receptionist. Despite some thirty years experience in 'community relations' the stereotyping I had learned in the distant past kicked in to produce assumptions which still control my mind. An American friend, Revd Joe Agne, talks about the tapes that play inside our heads. There are certain music tapes we know from the past which, even when we have not played them for a couple of years, we know automatically which song comes next, all the way through. 'The same goes for my racism', says Agne, 'I have tapes that play even at the most unexpected times. They are well-learned tapes..... they say weird things: They say, "African American people are violent and I should be afraid". Never mind that most of the violence in the world is perpetrated and supported by white persons. My tapes say, "If white kids are on a corner, it's a group of kids. If African American kids or Puerto Rican kids are on a corner, it's a gang". My tapes say, "African Americans are only good in sports and entertaining". Never mind that they are among our leading politicians, business people and clergy. My tapes say' "Native Americans are savages, alcoholics". Never mind the savage practices and alcoholism of the white community.' Agne talks of the need for white people to recognise that they can only be 'recovering racists', that the sense of superiority in us is so strong that it can never be eradicated, just - if we are alert - kept under control. One of the most effective therapies is to listen to black and minority people talk honestly about how they see things, that is really listen, do not interrupt and be willing to believe what they say. At the level of the church we have to recognise the pervasiveness of institutional racism. The Inquiry in Southwark Diocese referred to above reminded me of this; the assumed and effortless superiority of race and class of Anglican office-holders; the inflexibility of the expectations of style and method of leadership; the lack of representation of minorities in positions of influence; the stated inability, with requisite head-shaking, to find people of the 'right mix of skills and experience'. The pain of black people constantly faced with invisibility; the head-scratching accompanying statistics demonstrating boards and committees with one, two or no people from minorities in a Diocese where thousands of them attend church every Sunday. The Church needs to engage prophetically with what happens to black and minority people. It needs to do this at local level, looking for the issues in which it might engage, doing some modest research, then tackling the structures as to what might be done. In the Southwark Inquiry we were told about one neighbourhood where in the past racism had held sway, both in the local community and the local authority. This had been observed by some in the Churches, but it was not clear that more than one or two individuals had challenged this situation in any real way. We were told of another community where gypsies and travelling people sometimes stopped. They were strongly disliked by the local people and pressure was put on to the powers-that-be to move them on. The local church had not thought of making the point publicly that authorities in areas where travellers stop had a responsibility to provide some kind of site and services - otherwise the children would never go to school, health would remain poor, rubbish would not be collected and stereotyping and anti-social behaviour would continue indefinitely.

The Church also needs to act at national level. In the aftermath of the 1985 Broadwater Farm uprising in north London, when a police officer was savagely killed, three young men - two black, one of mixed ethnic background – were convicted of his murder. After investigation and discussion with local church leaders the Community and Race Relations Unit of the old British Council of Churches concluded this was a miscarriage of justice and joined the campaign to free the men. It was not popular, in the Churches or outside, but with the support of some church leaders, including one former Primus of the Scottish Episcopal Church, C.R.R.U. held to its support and was eventually vindicated when the men were released and two police officers charged with falsifying evidence. C.R.R.U. became the Churches Commission for Racial Justice, and continued to seek to represent the prophetic stance of the Churches against racism. For several years its Vice-Moderator was that same former Primus.

At 'national level', whatever that means in devolving Britain, the challenges continue. Many see the Immigration and Asylum Act, intended to become law in November 1999, as built on the continuing racism of British immigration control. Many are deeply disappointed that despite numerous efforts the 1976 Race Relations Act remains unamended and weak. Many are angry that unemployment among young black men is still far higher than that among young white men. There is rage in the black and minority communities that despite the Stephen

Lawrence Inquiry, and all that went with it; reports still emerge of black people being victimised by some police officers. A disproportionate number of black youngsters are both under-achieving in and being excluded from our schools. There are still high numbers of minorities in prisons and mental hospitals, and we seem unable to do anything about it.

Certain newspapers would suggest that the last paragraph is all driven by 'political correctness', in terms of identifying ethnic origin as a cause. They would say in today's Britain ethnic origin is not a problem, that if people try to get into Britain illegally, or have no qualifications, or misbehave or do not work at school, they will suffer for it, whatever their colour. They would like to persuade us that the playing field is already level, that there is nothing further that could or should be done, that there is no need for positive action to give everyone in the United Kingdom a genuinely equal opportunity. Their changes would be superficial and cosmetic. Christians need constantly to go beyond the clever but confusing jibes of political correctness. We need to focus on the dimensions of justicial correctness, to level the playing field, and on theological correctness, to explain why. As we do so we will find ourselves comrades in the struggle with those from the minority communities, many other Christians among them. We will also be 'doing the Gospel'.

Footnotes
[1] CARF (Campaign Against Racism and Fascism) bulletin, April/May 1999
[2] Race for the Millennium, David Haslam, Church House Publishing, 1996.
[3] ibid, p.11
[4] The Wood Sheppard Principles, Race Equality in Employment Project,
   c/o Christ Church, 27 Blackfriars Road, London SE1 8N

Bonhoeffer and the Poets

Rowan Williams

On a Sunday in April 1945, Dietrich Bonhoeffer conducted a service for his fellow prisoners, preaching on the texts, 'With his stripes we are healed' and 'Blessed be the God and father of our Lord Jesus Christ! By his great mercy we have been born anew to a living hope through the resurrection of Jesus from the dead'. Very shortly after the service ended, he was told to prepare for his last journey; before leaving the country schoolhouse in Bavaria where he and others had been held during Easter week, Bonhoeffer – famously – sent his last message, to Bishop George Bell, the message beginning, 'This is the end – for me the beginning of life'.

It was a typically paradoxical message, sent by a typical (but how unusual) German theologian to a typical (but how unusual) Anglican dignitary. The unlikely friendship between these two figures is something of a parable, a sign of two worlds communicating. What Bell meant to Bonhoeffer and what he might now mean to the world Bonhoeffer represented, the world of the directly experienced torment of twentieth century Europe, is not something we can talk about here: it is for our European fellow-Christians to tell us in due course, if we are ready to learn from them and listen to them. And the Anglican Church in these islands, it has to be said, has not got a wonderful record in listening and learning where the reformed churches of Europe are concerned. What we can reflect on is the message Bonhoeffer sends to us; and what I shall be suggesting is that, with a few exceptions, we are not happy with its paradoxical character and are always out to tame it. How easily Bonhoeffer could be made the patron of a rather bland liberalism, in the hands of an Anglo-Saxon public; how smoothly he seems to fit into preoccupations about human autonomy, about the inaccessibility of traditional doctrinal language, about the coming restructuring of the Church. Yet, once we read him more patiently and attentively, how awkward and even crass such a reading comes to appear, and how we are haunted by his difficulty. Those (quite a few) who had their primary exposure to Bonhoeffer through the quotations in John Robinson's *Honest to God* might be forgiven for reading him as a Christian revisionist and perhaps as an optimist about the modern condition. But Robinson's work was at least a serious attempt to translate Bonhoeffer, even if, in many ways, it represented a misunderstanding. More worrying was the translation offered by an American 'Death of God' theologian like William Hamilton, who, in an essay on Bonhoeffer written in 1965, rendered Bonhoeffer's plea for 'religionless Christianity as 'a plea to give up all claims for the necessity of religion generally. Christianity…is merely one of the possibilities available to man in a competitive and pluralistic spiritual situation today'[1]. Turn from this bland consumerism to Bonhoeffer's letter of summer 1944 and you know you are in a different universe – the passion to know God at the centre of strength as well as weakness, yet the passion to understand the weakness of the God who suffers being marginal, the God to whom *we* must go in compassion, to share his weakness.

But the puzzles remain. What is the meaning of that tantalising phrase, 'religion-less Christianity'? What might Bonhoeffer have said about 'the secular interpretation of biblical concepts' on July 8th, 1944 if the temperature had been cooler ('Well, it's time to say something concrete about the secular interpretation of biblical concepts; but it's too hot!')?[2] Strictly theological discussion continues. But Bonhoeffer is not the preserve of theologians; and in this lecture I want to listen to another way of receiving and wrestling with Bonhoeffer. At least three significant poets of the last decades have written about him, and their writing brings sharply into focus the difficulties of his work and the temptations of resolving something a bit too quickly. This is the writing about Bonhoeffer I want to reflect on; what message from the schoolhouse at Schönberg has come through on imagination, not just the intellect? And I ask that question in the confidence that Bishop Bell might well have approved, Bell who was one of the most generous patrons of religious art in the modern Church of England.

Jack Clemo's poetry is itself a difficult and contested legacy. The relentless Calvinist perspective of his earliest work, the images that speak almost of a sadism of grace, the destructive intrusion of the divine, like the scars of industrial desolation in a landscape, is as powerful as it is ambiguous and troubling – ambiguous because of its deliberate moral brinkmanship and aesthetic self-subversion. And even in the later and more measured poems, there remains a troubling self-conscious insistence on the difficulties of a personal history and a temperamental savagery of imagination – intelligible enough, God knows, for a man afflicted with blindness and deafness for most of his adult life. There is a pull back to self-dramatising; but increasingly this is itself reined in by a sceptical distancing from the 'brooding ego' and the rhetoric of isolation and bitter superiority. Clemo's 1986 collection, *A Different Drummer*,[3] contains a large number of poems on individuals, a feature that itself shows a particular strategy of discipline; one of these is devoted to Bonhoeffer.

> *Crooked cross on the muffed, tolled acre*
> *Told death's reign in iron, barbed wire,*
> *Bullet and crematoria smoke.*

Buchenwald of ill fame (faded
After thirty years' post-Nazi slime, the shame
of man's coming of age) displayed its back-drag
Into primeval nurseries. Bully and victim
Naked as in their first, fenced twilight; robe or rag
Of reason was torn, leaving snarl and slobber.
Even the faith-tongued, wilting amid vermin,
Felt the rosary rot while the gallows hemp stayed strong,
And the slammed hypothesis of a loving Maker
Echoed mockingly through the gurgling skein.

The young pastor with the poet's eyes
Kept his secret, musing calmly apart,
Tracing transcendence in the base day's dole.
Thoughts wrung from Hegel, Goethe, Barth
Flocked with clear peace of the Danube summer,
Bavarian forests in the free years, and warmer ties
Edging to poignancy; the girl he would never wed
Vanishing from the cell door at Tegel.....

The true Cross turned crooked under pressure:
His lovely trust and prayers knotted confusedly
With the cool brain's warp.
Blind guesses would stumble
Beyond the camp barrier, touching religious man,
Who seemed spilled, drained of creed-props,
over broken countries,
Shrugging at gutted churches. The captive pastor
Saw a Cross that meant mere crumpled deity,
A heaven that knew only secular service
From the adult nature's autonomy,

The camp gates opened in savage rain
For Bonhoeffer's final journey.

The truck rattled on besides the stung Danube
Under trees that did not rattle; the month was April,
With hushed knots of leaves and buds
passively bowing.
And he knelt at Flossenburg,
the last plank straight again
To his acquitted faith. An infinite mercy,
Moving above death-cell and execution yard,
Annulled for him the blind probe
And the secular tolling.

This is not, I think, one of Clemo's best poems, though it has all his usual energy and some very strongly realised moments – the 'slammed hypothesis of a loving Maker', for example, evokes the slammed door and the trap beneath the gallows as well as the colloquial sense of 'slam' as 'assault' or 'violently criticise'; the rain on the 'stung Danube' is vivid; and the 'secular tolling' at the end is a neat and effective retrieval of the opening image, the 'tolled acre' that is both the graveyard ('God's acre' in archaic usage) under the bells, and the territory that requires toll to be paid, requires the surrender of something. But overall the poem seems too determined to find a resolution. The opening section already prejudges the issue of 'man come of age': this must be an illusion; the nightmare of the Third Reich is surely a reversion to a Calvinist infancy, a realm of raging passion that reflects only the sin we are born to. The second section ('The young pastor with the poet's eyes....') is a curious, faintly sentimental picture that gives little ground for the drastic movement that follows, the transition to the buckled or crushed vision that eventually emerges in Bonhoeffer's 1944 letters; though, given Clemo's own passionate convictions about the need for erotic completion if the vision of God is to find speech in us, the convictions unforgettably spelled out in his autobiographical writing, the reference to 'the girl he would never wed' here is in fact more wistful 'colouring'[4]. But the pattern that appears in the poem is one that seems to assume that the prison letters represent confusion, even temptation. The mind, forced into a sort of no-man's land outside the camp (but are we here to think also of Christ's death 'outside the camp', in the language of the Letter to the Hebrews?), has become *blind*, and it is the '*captive* pastor' who sees the defeat of God and a heaven asking no more than 'secular service'. Bonhoeffer's martyrdom thus comes as a resolution of the torments of the letters. The 'hushed' leaves and the passivity of the spring buds suggest strongly that the acceptance of death restores the integrity of a faith under pressure. The bent cross straightens ('the last plank straight away/To his acquitted faith') and the blindness is removed, as is the 'secular tolling' – the world's demand for payment, for acceptance of its conditions, and the secular celebration of the death of God. The difficult passages of questioning are 'annulled'.

The central thesis here is not a glib or trivial one; but it risks imposing on Bonhoeffer a more simply *edifying* structure than either his life or his work might justify. Any hint of paradox is dissolved in a synthesis – a synthesis that admittedly is the most serious resolution there could be, a wholeness restored in silence, acceptance and death, yet one that requires us to read Bonhoeffer's uncertainties as transitional. I think – and I shall return to this – that there *is* a sense in which the culminating silence and death becomes an interpretation of the letters themselves; but this is rather different from treating the death as a *restoration* of what the letters lose or doubt (if anything, the contrary). Ultimately, Clemo's reading is of a very classically Calvinist character; this is a narrative of exemplary testing for faith. And it is difficult not to read in it also an element of assimilation of Bonhoeffer's struggle to Clemo's; is it entirely a matter of conventional imagery that the *blindness* of the probing mind is insisted upon? Clemo's autobiography details movingly the violent resentment and turbulence produced by the onset of blindness in his adolescence. The bending of souls to God's yoke, on the far side of affliction, is a recurrent theme in Clemo, and gives his religious poetry a gravity and toughness that is quite distinctive, even when also disturbing, since, as I've already noted, it suggests its own dismantling. The point is made in another poem in the same collection of Clemo's, 'A Choice about Art', which commemorates Oswald Chambers, painter turned evangelist.[5] Clemo points the moral that this is a progression reversing that of Van Gogh, whose espousal of 'the sun's rank relish for colour' in preference to the imperatives of the Kingdom leads finally to a restriction, even an exile from the depths of human experience under God. In a typical and typically bold and exultant image, the poem concludes that in Chambers' evangelistic labours and his marriage, 'A paradox barred to your old art groups, barred to Van Gogh, now bared its body and teemed'. The triumphant, almost savage, undercutting of the artist's achievement as such, in the name simultaneously of erotic fidelity and the gospel, says clearly that art, including the poem itself as it speaks, is at best a path into the deaths of commitment and risk for God's sake. And perhaps a good poem is one that pushes us nearer such death; in which case, the Bonhoeffer poem enacts rather more starkly than most a progression that all Christian poetry must follow. The questionings of the prison letters are like the complexities of art, a hunger (blind?) for what God will not give his elect – except when they bend passively to his decree, and find their crooked desires thus made straight.

Bonhoeffer was a Lutheran not a Calvinist; and I wonder how much Clemo's powerful misunderstanding of Bonhoeffer has to do with this. It is characteristic of Luther's own rhetoric to play with paradoxes, many of which have made theologians anxious for centuries. *Some* of Bonhoeffer's complexities undoubtedly spring from a natural affinity with Luther – the willingness to put together the God at the centre and the God at the edge, the strength of the human agent and the radical need of the human agent, faith and religionlessness, the experience of hell and the awareness of an unwelcome maturity. This is the language that cannot comfortably be reduced to the story of a Reformed saint any more than to the theorising of a liberal born out of due time. Yet the idea of a death that resolves, makes sense and so communicates remains intensely attractive, even to a writer who does not begin from a Calvinist standpoint. Geoffrey Hill must count as one of the most outstanding and haunting voices in contemporary English poetry, and part of his compelling quality for a religious leader lies in his continuing appropriation of and distancing from the imagery of Catholic Christian tradition. It is not surprising to find him writing about Bonhoeffer.[6]

'CHRISTMAS TREES'

Bonhoeffer in his skylit cell
bleached by the flares' candescent fall,
pacing out his own citadel,

Restores the broken themes of praise,
encourages our borrowed days,
by logic of his sacrifice.

Against wild reasons of the state
his words are quiet but not too quiet.
we hear too late or not too late.

The contrast with Clemo is sharp, in style as well as in substance. Even by Hill's own standards, this is a compressed poem, its surface elegance encoding a highly complex argument and almost diverting attention from a very deliberate non-resolution. The prison cell is a 'citadel', a place of refuge or defence; but not a place defended from the violence of contemporary culture, as it is lit by the 'flares' of wartime. Flares go up at night: so the light that comes into this cell from the sky is the artificial radiance of a night of battle, fear, tension. His illumination is in, not outside, the violence; and the 'pacing out' of the citadel suggests both the pacing out of foundations, measurements, for a building, and the anxious pacing of confinement. But this act of 'founding' a place of refuge (and the language of 'founding' is important to Hill in other poems, notably in the fifth of the *Lachrimae* sequence of sonnets in the same collection) is a restoration of the possibilities of praise, construction in the middle of chaos, which, reminding us that our time is not our own ('our borrowed days'), establishes a human space over against totalitarianism, against the 'wild', inhuman, logic of the total and overriding priority of national interest. In the background is the classical French phrase, 'raison d'état', which designates a political interest that is capable of supplanting certain moral concerns; the concept was discussed more than once by the late Donald MacKinnon, a Christian philosopher enormously important for Hill, and a glance at MacKinnon's major essay of 1974 on this subject is illuminating.[7] 'Raison d'état is what dictates actions designed to preserve some kind of organisation of common life under law, an organised life endowed with the power to defend itself[8]; but it is always on the edge of so justifying *any* action designed to preserve state authority and the rule of law that it risks undermining the rule of law itself. MacKinnon refers in conclusion to the St Bartholomew's Eve massacre in sixteenth century France, as an instance of the failure of a rational politics and the triumph of violence in the defence of the state, in such a way that the state itself becomes infected with a pervasive violent lawlessness in virtue of its defence, even its 'grounding' in injustice. And it is far from irrelevant here to think of Bishop Bell's protest against the pursuance of just war by unjust means, a protest which Donald MacKinnon regarded as paradigmatic.

Hill sets logic against logic: the 'reason of the state' appealed to by totalitarians has lost its sanity, become irretrievably violent, and another rationality must be invoked – the 'logic of his sacrifice', the rationality of Bonhoeffer's death. Or so it seems; but one might wonder whether the 'sacrifice' is something broader and more ambivalent, the giving up of an uninvolved or innocent position. Given Hill's anguished awareness of the betrayals and distortions of the poet's own enterprise, as well as his fascination with the theme of blood-sacrifice (expressed particularly in his early collection, *For the Unfallen*, sacrifice that, in its violence, establishes a compelling but destructive image or order, we might want to read the lines on Bonhoeffer more carefully. The sacrifice that restores the possibility of praise (a theme redolent of Auden on Yeats) is both a real death and the death of innocence involved in action and speech, that death of innocence accepted by Bonhoeffer in his collusion with the plot for Hitler's assassination. For Bonhoeffer, the risk is somehow vindicated: 'his words are quiet but not too quiet'. As one commentator[9] has observed, "'quiet' is a word to tense the ear" in Hill's poetry – something distinct from silence, something inviting an extremity of attention". 'Quiet but not too quiet' catches simultaneously the necessary quiet, the tension of the speaker, agent, poet himself or herself, and the necessary clarity and risk involved in being active at all, in self-determination. Bonhoeffer, after all, is in his prison cell under the flares precisely because of risky and in some ways morally disputable options, and the words he utters from that cell are risky – as well as humble and attentive – reflections. Another writer discussing Hill [John Bayley] adds that 'The authority of poetry is always 'too late', because it cannot coincide with the fact it seeks to immortalise'. *Any* words are going to be 'too late', compromised, involved in the violence of the ego that presents itself in such words. But 'not too late' as well; somehow Bonhoeffer has a language that does not disconnect us from what the same critic calls the 'original contingency and imperfection that goes with original intensity and anguish'. Bonhoeffer's unfinishedness – a life cut short, a theological scheme left in fragments – is exactly what holds up for us a logic that will resist the omnipotent administrative state, the logic of *dispossession*, letting go of a certain kind of justification, a certain kind of intelligibility or fluency.

Like Clemo, then, Hill sees Bonhoeffer as an exemplar of surrender; but where Clemo thinks in terms of surrender to the will of God, involving the abandonment of dangerous thoughts, Hill sees the 'sacrifice' as the acceptance of what these dangerous thoughts entail, a saintly surrendering of easy innocence. And the effect of the sacrifice is the founding or re-founding of both a politics and a language. Over against the self-destruction of violence and the corruption of language that comes with political tyranny, Bonhoeffer restores the honesty of 'quiet' – the self-interrogating and ultimately self-dispossessing voice and style that becomes in some way transparent to some other and deeper agency or presence: a speech for God; praise. Hill takes us a good deal further into Bonhoeffer's Lutheran paradoxes than Clemo, with these hints about the difficulty of honest speech and action. But it is interesting that both Hill and Clemo are drawn to write about Bonhoeffer in a way that suggests, however obscurely, that they are *writing about themselves writing,* as well as about the ways there might be of writing poetry that is serious about God. For both, such seriousness is to be enacted in the poetry's dismantling of itself or subversion of itself. Clemo sees the poetry of faith as pushing towards something uncompromisingly beyond mere 'art'; Hill, not exactly a poet of 'faith' yet unmistakeably a poet obsessed with God, more subtly invites us to listen for words that become open to God (and remain open to God) by their non-insistent but yet intense and attentive quality, a quality that can be shown in non-resolution. It is not a non-resolution born of unclarity and uncertainty, but a gesture towards the other who is the object of praise and who is thus (literally) infinitely more important than the 'finish' of the words; the close surface of a well-formed utterance looks not towards the object of praise but towards the human and corrupting audience. It is a typical paradox that Hill articulates this in a *technically* brilliantly finished form.

But if Bonhoeffer restores the language of praise, can we say anything about the God who appears, who shows himself, in the gestures of such talk? The third poem I want to examine, the longest and in many ways the most complex of all, is the one that is least involved in writing about writing (at first reading anyway) and most concerned with the hidden-ness and the self-showing of God: W.H. Auden's 'Friday's Child',[10] written probably in 1958, nearer the event of Bonhoeffer's death than either of the poems I have so far been looking at, and (very significantly) prior to the rather half-hearted discovery of Bonhoeffer by liberal theology. It is distinctive in all kinds of ways, but not least in preserving the quite unliberal starkness of Bonhoeffer himself. I think it is one of the greatest religious poems in English this century.

Friday's Child
(In memory of Dietrich Bonhoeffer, martyred at Flossenburg, April 9th, 1945)

He told us we were free to choose
But, children as we were, we thought-

208

'Paternal Love will only use
Force in the last resort.

On those too bumptious to repent'-
Accustomed to religious dread.
It never crossed our minds He meant
Exactly what He said.

Perhaps He frowns, perhaps He grieves,
But it seems idle to discuss
If anger or compassion leaves
The bigger bangs to us.

What reverence is rightly paid
To a Divinity so odd
He lets the Adam whom He made
Perform the Acts of God?

It might be jolly if we felt
Awe at this Universal Man
(When kings were local, people knelt);
Some try to, but who can?

The self-observed observing Mind
We meet when we observe at all
Is not alarming or unkind
But utterly banal.

Though instruments at Its command
Make wish and counter-wish come true,
It clearly cannot understand
What It can clearly do.

Since the analogies are rot
Our senses based belief upon

We have no means of learning what
Is really going on.

And must put up with having learned
All proofs or disproofs that we tender
Of His existence are returned
Unopened to the sender

Meanwhile, a silence on the cross,
As dead as we shall ever be,
Speaks of some total gain or loss.
And you and I are free.

To guess from the insulted face
Just what Appearances He saves
By suffering in a public place
A death reserved for slaves.

The childish religious mind, 'Accustomed to religious dread', tends to conceive the freedom bestowed on us by God as something provisional and temporary, undergirded by a safety net in the assurance that 'Paternal Love' still reserves the power to bring about its will by force. But what if the divine renunciation of violence is completely serious? In that case, there is no point in wondering whether it is in anger or in pity that God stands back from the world or reacts to what the world does: he has elected powerlessness in the terms of the world. Even if there was a 'Big Bang' to initiate the universe, we are left to make the 'bigger bangs' of self-determination, creating as if we were God. But this human image of God, endowed with this liberty of shaping the world as it wills, is a disappointment. The power of the adult mind, the universalising reason of modernity, does not command reverence: the wonderful line, 'When kings were local, people knelt' speaks (accurate) volumes about perceptions of authority in a modernity that is without specific loyalties and traditional commitments. 'Adult' self-awareness is not frightening but 'banal'.

Auden is strikingly prophetic here. The portrait of the post-enlightenment mind, preoccupied with 'instrumental reason' and stranded without adequate self-knowledge is in itself pointed enough; but the use of the word 'banal' will evoke for many readers Hannah Arendt's phrase about the 'banality of evil' as applied to the professional bureaucrats of the Third Reich. Arendt's great essay on *Eichmann in Jerusalem,* in which this idea was first developed, did not appear until 1963; Auden was reading her book, *The Human Condition* in 1959,[11] and recognised in it certain themes close to his own deepest preoccupations. He was corresponding with Arendt at the time of her reflections on the Eichmann trial, and it is not too fanciful to suppose that the banality of the rootless instrumental mind sketched by Auden in this poem was one of the elements in Arendt's dissection of the peculiarly modern variety of evil represented by the faithful and competent administrator in a totalitarian system. This is obviously to move beyond what the poem itself says; but Arendt's vision of totalitarian rationality casts its shadow before it in these lines, and it is hard to read them without that shadow in view.

What does modern, banal, reason not understand ('It clearly cannot understand/ What it can clearly do')? We have been told that what reasoning humanity can do is to 'Perform the Acts of God'; but there is a manifest irony here. The Instrumental reason of modernity can 'Make wish and counterwish come true', in a kind of parody of omnipotence: as if the ultimate power were wish-fulfilment. This *looks* like the act of God. But the act which the poem commemorates at its opening is the act of self-resignation to the freedom of the other; and this the banal mind doesn't and can't grasp. Its position is made worse by the fact that what once propped up belief no longer works; there is not even the basis for the kind of picture of God that might at least introduce us to the narrative of self-abnegating creation. The reality of what is going on is hidden. And Auden offers one of his most memorable conceits in the image of the proofs of divine existence 'Returned/ Unopened to the sender', only to give it a brilliant extra twist with 'did he really break the seal...?' If the resurrection were indeed a visible demonstration of divine power, we should have a reply to our enquiries about God, a proof of sorts. But 'we' dare not say: Auden doesn't tell us, of course, who 'we' are, but it seems to be believers as opposed to the 'conscious unbelievers' of the line following. Believers are embarrassed and tongue-tied about the empty tomb, while unbelievers are secure in their confidence in the verdict that will finally be passed on their lives (I take it that this is how we should read this rather tantalising pair of lines: it could be that the unbelievers are sure about the *reality* of the Judgment Day, but this makes less sense).

There follows a quite extraordinary change of key. The poem's compressed, epigrammatic, dry and sardonic tones give way to a no less compressed and elusive register, but one in which entire seriousness takes over. There are no proofs; there is no visibly broken seal, no manifest interruption of the ignorance of the omnicompetent and helpless modern reason. There is a silence that speaks for God, for the 'total gain or loss' that is God's action of self-losing for the sake of created freedom. The skilful *enjambement* of 'free/ To guess...' leaves us with the hint that freedom is what results from the 'total gain or loss' of the crucifixion, while carrying us on to a further turn of the argument. We are free to guess, not compelled to see; but we *might* guess the fundamental paradox of all as we reflect on God's enduring of a 'death reserved for slaves'. The Aristotelean saving of appearances, the hermeneutical principle that no interpretation should require us to ignore what is actually present to our senses, dictates that the cross should not be simply another of those analogies that once, misleadingly, suggested belief to our senses. The saving of appearances here is the fact that the cross leaves everything as it is (as Wittgenstein said of philosophy); its very silence, its non-intervention in the way of this world, is its mode of communicating what is otherwise incommunicable, the freedom of God in the act of creating and the unfreedom of God in the world that is created. If God is truly the creator of the world, there is no point in the world that *is* God; God must be absent. If God truly creates a free world, God can appear in the world only as a slave, as what he is not. Auden knew his Kierkegaard as well as his Bonhoeffer, and what is sketched here is very close indeed to Kierkegaard's account of what must be involved in the revelation of God in the world, the 'absolute paradox' of the *Philosophical Fragments.* And this in turn looks back to Luther's vision of divine revelation in what is radically other than God. Only so does the sheer difference of God show itself, the truth that God cannot *correspond* to some form of worldly appearance.

Auden's Bonhoeffer challenges us to think about the modern mind's ignorance of itself – an odd charge, at first sight, to lay at the door of a modernity so obsessed with interpretation and self-interpretation, with suspicion and reductive analyses. But this Bonhoeffer accuses us of not knowing whose image we are made in, the image of a freedom so unqualified it can make of itself a slave, a word so full that can make of itself a silence. We exist because of God's willed, created silence before what is other; the other made by God is left to 'Perform the Acts of God' unconstrained by a parental hand, and systematically misconstrues those acts as acts of control and of the satisfaction of desires. But the revealed act of God in the cross shows what freedom it is that we might aspire to if we listen. We can create silence in front of the other, we can silence the ignorant noise of the ego, the banality of self-regard that can so simply and easily slip into violence or tyranny. If this leaves us, like God incarnate, in the form of a slave by the world's standards, so be it. As Bonhoeffer no doubt appreciated, jolting in the truck between Schönberg and Flossenbûrg, the renunciation is both total gain and total loss ('This is the end – for me the beginning of life').

All three of my chosen poets end up by intimating that talking about God has to be a kind of death. Clemo sees this in the clearest and most traditional terms: martyrdom is an end to ambiguity, a paradigm act of obedience to divine sovereignty. Rebellion is an intelligible and perhaps unavoidable testing of commitment, but the simplicity of the gallows 'annuls' the previous questioning. The death asked of us is a letting go of the controls of art, the skills of imagination, which can be used only to bring us to an edge where the decision is clear. Unlike – say – George Herbert, another poet with a strong Calvinist undertow, Clemo does not seem to allow that the enactment *in* language of the pain or bewilderment of speaking of God can itself function as a testimony to the triumph of grace, in and not beyond the 'probing'. Hill, in contrast, is interested in precisely the 'sacrifice' that involves the whole of Bonhoeffer's speech and action, the restoration of proper language for God in the words of a compromised speaker and agent who, in accepting the 'death' of ambiguity achieves a quiet that is just sufficiently, precariously, audible in a time of corrupted culture and politics. The sacrifice of intelligent, self-aware, penitent acceptance of the finite world, with its risks of lying and sin in every moment, is foundational for an adequate defence against the pseudo-rationality of violent self-maintenance. Only in a precise but conscientiously open or unfinished language, nudging us towards the fundamental reality we can only rightly speak of in adoration, can we find the humility that will protect us from the seductions of totalitarianism. And Auden, picking up the same theme of rationalities, sane and insane, challenges enlightenment-instrumental reason to re-examine its own interiority (or lack of it) its impersonal, timeless and universal claims, which hide its nature from itself: the calling of human intelligence is indeed to become Godlike, but in attention and renunciation, not in making 'wish and counterwish come true'.

All three, writing about Bonhoeffer, manifestly write about themselves – about themselves writing, as I put earlier, about themselves as inheritors of the legacy of a corrupting century. And it is their awareness of writing about danger, corruption, in politics and culture and the language of faith that makes them, in the long run, better guides to Bonhoeffer than those theologians who have deployed his ideas without a sense of danger. Writing about martyrs ought to be a risky business; writing about a martyr whose martyrdom is involved in a story of compromised political action ought to be still riskier; and writing about a martyr who in his last twelve months recognised increasingly the noisy and self-regarding character of most theological utterances should intensify still further the peril of writing about him. But we ought to go on writing about him and being worried by him - above all by his diagnosis of the non-transformative nature of so much of our traditional doctrinal idiom, This is the most readily misunderstood bit of his thinking, because it suggests that one set of unsatisfactory words can be replaced by new and more intelligible expressions; whereas his challenge cuts to a deeper *moral* level, to the level of our uses of language, conservative or liberal or radical, to defend ourselves and our positions, to secure advantages. Bonhoeffer asks what talking about God might be like if we forgot about *gaining advantage*, over our opponents in theological debate, over the presumed weakness of the unbeliever (who often remains 'Quite sure

215

of Judgment Day' and impervious to our attempts to convict him or her of their need for assurance before their maker), over God himself. If we could discover that, we might be nearer the transfigurative heart of speech about God. But to write about this is, of course, to write about our own corruption, our readiness to speak for advantage; and that is hard.

If Hill – and, by implication, Auden – is right, working at this unanswerable question has some public resonance; it is not just an issue of concern to the religious minority. Politics needs the challenge of silence as much as does the Church, especially when the language of public life is increasingly corrupted by an obsession with 'advantage' – with all that that means for the silencing of the other, the refusal to seek oneself in the other, the inattention and wilful ignorance, that more and more stifles political *conversation*. A political discourse corrupted in such ways is already on the road to the anti-language of totalitarianism. Writing about Bonhoeffer is writing about our present political selves; and that is sufficiently uncomfortable for us perhaps to prefer a more manageably reformist Bonhoeffer.

And what if theology in particular has become the victim of this political corruptness, and operates more and more in terms of advantage? It has to be taught a different register, a different dialect, by writers who are more used to dealing in risk, perhaps. Any poet worth the name has learned to write from and to a place where advantage is not at issue – which is why poetry is profoundly political in its implications but profoundly resistant to political orthodoxy. If we find – as I'm suggesting – that poets may have more to say to us about Bonhoeffer at the moment than theologians, that is a function of the way in which the discourses currently work, and an invitation to theology to look again for a way of speaking that manages to embody something of dispossession and

216

disadvantage, whether this is in a more unashamed attention to the language of adoration or in a more sustained attempt to listen to and to speak with those who are directly and materially dispossessed – which is a different task from fashionable advocacy, radical chic, which is another kind of 'advantage' language.

And having written that, I find, of course, that Bonhoeffer wrote it first. 'Our being Christians today will be limited to two things: prayer and righteous action among [human being's]. Perhaps one of the most telling things in writing about a figure of Bonhoeffer's stature is the discovery that we are already written about in what we read.

Footnotes

[1] TJJ Attizer & W Hamilton, *Radical Theology & the Death of God*, Harmondsworth 1968, p.122
[2] *Letters & Papers from Prison* (enlarged edition), London 1971
[3] Padstow, 1986
[4] See especially Clemo's *Confession of a Rebel,* London 1949
[5] op.cit.,pp.20-21
[6] *Tenebrae*, London 1978, p.41
[7] Law, Change & Revolution: Some Reflections on the Concept of *Raison d'État, Exploration in Theology,* London 1979, pp.350-54
[8] op.cit., p.37
[9] Adrian Poole, *'Hill's version of Brand'* in P Robinson, ed., Geoffrey Hill. *Essays on his Work,* Milton Keynes 1985, p.97
[10] *Collected Poems*, London 1976, pp.509-510
[11] He reviewed it for *Encounter* in 1959

The Rag and Bone Shop of the Heart

Richard Holloway

A useful distinction used to be made between *natural theology* and *revealed theology*. The best way to work with the distinction is to think of an example. Let me tell you about the house in the woods. You are out walking in a wood, far from civilisation, when you come to a clearing in the forest, and in the midst of the clearing there is a cottage. It is clearly an inhabited dwelling, because everything seems to be in good order. There are curtains in the windows, a fire is burning in the grate of the living room and a large room at the back is clearly the study, comfortably littered with books and papers. The whole place testifies to the personality of the owner, though he or she is not present. Using common-sense and a flair for detective work, you can build up a picture of the owner from the evidence that lies all around you. A pipe-rack on the mantelpiece suggests to you that he, and it is likely to be a man, smokes a pipe. The hundreds of books that cram the cottage suggest a reader, a person of learning and study. The pictures on the wall and the careful attention to colour and design in the furnishings and decoration suggest someone for whom beauty and comfort are important. In this way, in the absence of the owner, using your natural reason, you build up a picture of the absent occupant. You have, in fact, engaged in a piece of natural theology, deducing from evidence that is present to your senses the existence, and something of the character, of the absentee owner, who is not present to your senses. The arguments for the existence of God used to follow that kind of procedure, Paley's watch being one of the most famous of the versions offered, in which the finder of a watch inferred from its presence on the beach the existence of a watch-maker. Most of the arguments from design were worked out before Darwin discovered the unimaginably long aeons of time required for the adaptation of species to their environment, and few people offer them as serious arguments today, but they do illustrate the distinction I am trying to explain.

It was held that, by our natural reason alone, we could infer or deduce the existence of God from the evidence our senses gave us of a created order that required a creator, a level of design that spoke of a designer, and the presence in our breasts of a conscience that pointed to the existence of a moral structure to the universe. From all of that a picture was built up of a God beyond us who was not available to our senses. However, there is something unsatisfying about a purely hypothetical cottage owner. We long for him to stride out of the forest and make himself known to us, invite us in for tea, and charm us with his conversation and wisdom. But we cannot be in control of that event; we can only be alert for it, and open to it when it occurs, when the revelation finally takes place. *Revealed theology*, therefore, is that knowledge of God that comes to us, it is claimed, from outside ourselves, from God, from beyond, and it tells us things about God that we could not deduce for ourselves. Revelations usually come through inspired individuals who are recognised as having been with God; and these sacred individuals either create, or there is created round them, writings that record the details of their disclosures. *Revealed* theology becomes the study of this body of material, and it is usually approached with greater reverence and care than *natural* theology, because it is held to be sacred in itself. Sometimes this reverence is expressed liturgically, as when, for example, the book of the Gospels is carried in procession and is incensed and kissed during the eucharist in the Christian Church; or when devout Moslems turn towards Mecca in their prayers, because Mecca

220

was the place of revelation to the Prophet and is, therefore, deemed to be a sacred place.

The difficulty with the traditional distinction between natural and revealed theology is that no qualitative difference actually exists between the two sources of theological data, apart from the particular honour that has been accorded to the allegedly revealed elements in theology. Even if we think there is something mysterious about the universe, and that it conveys some sense of latency or hidden presence, we have to admit that *everything* we know about it comes to us through our senses and is recorded by our senses. We may be watching a person praying in Church who is deep in communication with the invisible presence of God, but all that is available to us is the human, this-worldly side of that transaction. We can only hear the sound of one hand clapping, as it were, see the person on her knees, rapt in devotion, not the presence she is focused upon. This need not necessarily imply the non-existence of the invisible presence that is beyond discernment by our senses; it *does* imply that the only thing we can have access to is the bit that lies on this side of the interaction. Everything that is said or written about that interaction is inescapably human, made by us. The frustrating thing about this situation is that it usually leads to a futile conflict between those who believe in the transcendent origins of revelation and those who see it as a human activity of projection. Those who believe in revelation assert that it has come to them directly from God; those who believe that all religious claims can be explained in a naturalistic way dismiss their claim. What I want to suggest is that neither approach is really subtle enough to help us to engage with the mystery of discovery that, in theological shorthand, we call revelation. Moreover, the natural way of accounting for revelation need not be reductive; it may, in fact, increase our amazement at the mystery of its creativity.

Yet nature is made better by no mean,
But nature makes that mean: so o'er that art,
Which, you say, adds to nature, is an art
That nature makes...The art itself is nature.
                                    The Winter's Tale[IV.3]

I would like to propose that we replace the distinction between natural and revealed theology with a new distinction, which I would like to call mental theology and imaginative theology, or cerebral theology and emotional theology. We acknowledge that theology is a human activity, something *we* do, but we also acknowledge that it is done in different ways, rather like the distinction between right and left brain thinking. However we put it, we begin by acknowledging that all these mysterious discoveries come from us, are part of the extraordinary reality of human nature and its gift of consciousness. Our forebears described these mysteries in one way; we think about them in another way; what is common is the experience; what differs is the framework or template we create in order to express it. The reference frame of the biblical writers was a three-tier, flat universe, with heaven above, earth in the middle and hell or the underworld, literally beneath us. That is why there is all that spatial language in scripture about God being above us, and why when the hymn writers wanted to express something of the shock and newness of Jesus they said '*he came down to earth from heaven*'. We take that language metaphorically today. I am not absolutely convinced that they did not also understand it metaphorically in their day, but it is now a cause of some confusion for us. Marcus Borg has said that one of the problems for theology today is that some of us want to historicise or literalise what were always meant to be metaphors, thereby robbing us of a powerful and permanent way of using the biblical material. I can profitably use the metaphor of descent and ascent to describe the significance of Jesus; but if you insist that I take it literally, whatever you think you mean by that, then you deprive me of any valid and creative use of the biblical material. If we can move away from theology for a moment and look at another, related field of inspiration we might get a better understanding of the kind of distinction I am trying to make here. Let me say a few words about the Irish poet, W.B.Yeats.

When Yeats was an old man he thought that he had lost the gift of poetry. He brooded on the fact that, when younger, the images of inspiration, what he called his circus animals, had come to him unbidden from outside himself, by revelation, as it were; but now they seemed to have deserted him.

> *I sought a theme and sought for it in vain,*
> *I sought it daily for six weeks or so.*
> *Maybe at last being but a broken man*
> *I must be satisfied with my heart, although*
> *Winter and summer till old age began*
> *My circus animals were all on show.*

A new biography claims that many of Yeats' inspirations came from his fascination with the occult. Yeats was 51 when he married George Hyde-Lees on October 20 1917; his new wife was 21. It was a complex relationship, and there is plenty of evidence that Yeats was in love with someone else at the time. What cemented the relationship, at any rate during its early years, was George's facility for automatic writing. This fascinated Yeats; indeed, Brenda Maddox, author of, *George's Ghosts*, the biography in question, suggests that his young wife contrived the arrangement, probably unconsciously, in order to capture her husband's interest, and that she continued to use it to direct the relationship, particularly in the sexual department. After all, a 51 year old man, just married, probably needs prompting to embark upon fatherhood, and what better coach could there be for someone who was fascinated by and passionately believed in the occult than a friendly ghost? But George's ghosts provided more than sexual encouragement and advice on domestic arrangements; they provided powerful images that went into some of Yeats most famous poems. Here is a passage from Maddox's fascinating book.

'In January 1919 Yeats completed what is probably the best-known poem of his later years, 'The Second Coming'. Incorporating the symbols he had been receiving through the Script (the automatic writing his wife was doing at his request) *since his marriage, it could not have been more timely.*

Europe was reeling from the effects of the war. From Russia Bolshevism cast its shadow over the old patterns of work. War had broken out between the sexes. Ireland was on the brink of rebellion and within Irish society the Protestant Ascendancy had lost its grip. The old order was dead. Yeats' poem encompassed it all:

Turning and turning in the widening gyre
The falcon cannot hear the falconer;
Things fall apart; the centre cannot hold;
Mere anarchy is loosed upon the world,
The blood-dimmed tide is loosed, and   everywhere
The ceremony of innocence is drowned;
The best lack all conviction, while the worst
Are full of passionate intensity.'

Maddox points out that this extraordinary poem is strong enough to accommodate all the meanings that have been read into it: historical, political, religious and scientific. Then she goes on to offer what she calls an obstetrical interpretation. I quote it here, not necessarily because I agree with it, but because it shows how revelatory texts are open to many interpretations and become larger than their original meaning or intention. She writes:

> 'His personal life, with its newly established order, was menaced by the 'shape with lion body and the head of a man' advancing towards him in George's expanding belly. Very soon, after a burst of water and blood, he would be 'vexed to nightmare by a rocking cradle', deprived of the total attention of his wife on whom he had come to depend, torn by primitive jealousies he had long fought to bury and disturbed by squalling noise when he needed absolute silence for writing poetry. After the unstoppable beast's arrival, the one certain thing is that his life will never be the same again.

> The Second Coming! Hardly are those words out
> When a vast image out of **Spiritus Mundi**
> Troubles my sight: somewhere in the sands
> of the desert
> A shape with lion body and the head of a man,
> A gaze blank and pitiless as the sun,
> Is moving its slow thighs, while all about it
> Reel shadows of the indignant desert birds.
> The darkness drops again; but now I know
> That twenty centuries of stony sleep
> Were vexed to nightmare by a rocking cradle
> And what rough beast,
> its hour come round at last,
> Slouches towards Bethlehem to be born'.[1]

The main point here is not the cogency of any particular piece of Yeatsian interpretation, but the fact that Yeats, at this stage in his career, would have claimed that his poetic symbols, his inspiration, came from another world, a realm outside himself, *The Second Coming*, being a potent example of that revelatory process. But here he is, an old man, unable to compose, his circus animals all on strike, refusing to visit him. Gradually, he realises that it was, all along, his own heart that was the source of his inspiration, and not some exalted sphere beyond himself. So he realises he must get back inside himself, back to where all the ladders of effort and inspiration start, like someone struggling to lift himself out of a slum. The poem ends:

> '*Now that my ladder's gone*
> *I must lie down where all the ladders start*
> *In the foul rag and bone shop of the heart.*'

I think Yeats' experience offers us a way of understanding how inspiration or revelation really works, no matter what frame of reference we use to describe it, whether supernatural or occult. All the ladders start in the human heart; we generate the material; we create the images; the art comes through us or, to be more precise, through people of genius, inspired individuals. Using that as an approach, I want to look at two passages from the New Testament, both from the Acts of the Apostles, that will help us think about the meaning and processes of revelation, of those new discoveries we go on making about our own nature and the nature of the universe. The first passage is about Paul's conversion on the road to Damascus, from chapter 9, verses 1 - 9:

> *[9:1] Meanwhile Saul, still breathing threats and murder against the disciples of the Lord, went to the high priest [2] and asked him for letters to the synagogues at Damascus, so that if he found any who belonged to the Way, men or women, he might bring them bound to*

Jerusalem. [3] Now as he was going along and approaching Damascus, suddenly a light from heaven flashed around him. [4] He fell to the ground and heard a voice saying to him, "Saul, Saul, why do you persecute me?" [5] He asked, "Who are you, Lord?" The reply came, "I am Jesus, whom you are persecuting. [6] But get up and enter the city, and you will be told what you are to do." [7] The men who were traveling with him stood speechless because they heard the voice but saw no one. [8] Saul got up from the ground, and though his eyes were open, he could see nothing; so they led him by the hand and brought him into Damascus. [9] For three days he was without sight, and neither ate nor drank.

Remembering where all the ladders start, in the foul rag and bone shop of the heart, how can we interpret this interesting story? A literalistic reading would claim, as Saul himself did on subsequent occasions, that he was on the receiving end of a divine intervention. He was riding along on the road to Damascus when a light from outside himself blinds him and a voice, also from outside, commands him to cease his persecution of the followers of Jesus. We read in the following verses that a follower of Jesus named Ananias comes to him and ministers to him, restoring his sight, and Saul, now to be called Paul, becomes a Christian apostle. There is no doubt that something happened to Saul of Tarsus that turned him into the apostle to the gentiles and the formative genius behind the early theological understanding of Jesus. We can accept all that, we can even accept the apparently miraculous blindness that afflicted him, but we do not need to depart from the human heart of Saul to explain it all. The occasion of a conversion may be a single moment in time, but we know enough about the human heart to realise that the single moment was prepared for by a process, however unconscious, that was already going on. Saul's passionate vehemence against the followers of Jesus would suggest that his attention had already been arrested by the movement he was persecuting. This is a common phenomenon. We know enough about bigotry to understand something of its causality and one of its roots is fear or anxiety. The violent homophobe is often a man uncertain about and threatened by the unacknowledged whispers of his own sexuality. The classic way to deal with this kind of discomfort is to externalise or project it onto someone you can punish for the distress you feel about your own unadmitted longings. We call it scape-goating. Nietzsche captures it perfectly in the *Genealogy of Morals*:

> *'Every sufferer instinctively seeks a cause for his suffering; more exactly, an agent; still more specifically, a guilty agent who is susceptible to suffering - in short, some living thing upon, which he can, on some pretext or other, vent his affects, actually or in effigy: for the venting of his affects represents the greatest attempt on the part of the suffering to win relief,* **anaesthesia,** *the narcotic he cannot help desiring to deaden pain of any kind'* [2]

Nor need we leave the human heart of Saul to account for the apparently miraculous blindness that afflicted him. The blindness was probably psychogenic, a somatic expression of the turmoil in his soul, as he refused to acknowledge, refused to *see,* what his own heart was telling him: that Jesus of Nazareth had captured him for himself and would, if surrendered to, take over his entire life. The story of Paul's conversion, therefore, can be accounted for without recourse to supernatural agency; it was a struggle that was resolved within his own heart. And we see a similar process at work in the life of the other great apostle, Peter. In Acts chapter 10:

[10:1] In Caesarea there was a man named Cornelius, a centurion of the Italian Cohort, as it was called. [2] He was a devout man who feared God with all his household; he gave alms generously to the people and prayed constantly to God. [3] One afternoon at about three o'clock he had a vision in which he clearly saw an angel of God coming in and saying to him, "Cornelius." [4] He stared at him in terror and said, "What is it, Lord?" He answered, "Your prayers and your alms have ascended as a memorial before God. [5] Now send men to Joppa for a certain Simon who is called Peter; [6] he is lodging with Simon, a tanner, whose house is by the seaside." [7] When the angel who spoke to him had left, he called two of his slaves and a devout soldier from the ranks of those who served him, [8] and after telling them everything, he sent them to Joppa.

[9] About noon the next day, as they were on their journey and approaching the city, Peter went up on the roof to pray. [10] He became hungry and wanted something to eat; and while it was being prepared, he fell into a trance. [11] He saw the heaven opened and something like a large sheet coming down, being lowered to the ground by its four corners. [12] In it were all kinds of four-footed creatures and reptiles and birds of the air. [13] Then he heard a voice saying, "Get up, Peter; kill and eat." [14] But Peter said, "By no means, Lord; for I have never eaten anything that is profane or unclean." [15] The voice said to him again, a second time, "What God has made clean, you must not call profane." [16] This happened three times, and the thing was suddenly taken up to heaven.

A similar dynamic is at work in this story as in the story of Saul's conversion. The admission of the gentiles to the Jesus movement was clearly the most neuralgic issue in the life of the young community. James of Jerusalem, the brother or cousin of Jesus, was the conservative of the movement, who resisted any liberalising of the requirements of the Law upon devout Jews. The young church was a messianic movement within Judaism, a tendency, a sect even; but it had no pretensions to replace or go beyond Judaism, which the admission of the gentiles would effect. The new and zealous convert to the movement, still deeply mistrusted by its leadership, was the radical Paul, who believed that the new revelation of God that had come through Jesus had superseded the Law. And Peter, like many leaders anxious to preserve institutional unity, was caught in the middle. We can imagine the turmoil in which he lived and which even invaded his dreams. The fascinating thing about the dream of the sailcloth let down from heaven, containing creatures forbidden to a Jew, was that it represented a struggle in Peter's understanding of the authority of scripture, a subject that still torments believers. God had already forbidden the very creatures Peter was now being commanded to eat. Peter's dilemma is that he has a hunch God is now calling upon him to change his mind; God is revising God! Is scripture a word for all time or can it be revised, or our interpretation of it, to allow us to respond to new challenges and conditions? That is a very contemporary dilemma, but it was Peter's dilemma at Joppa. Again, we need not leave Peter's heart in order to account for the struggle and its resolutions: that's where all the ladders start. We know that Peter resolved the question, at any rate for the time being, when Cornelius came knocking on the door asking for baptism. And that, too, fits the dynamic of revelation. We struggle intellectually or psychologically with an abstract issue: can women be ordained? should gay and lesbian people be allowed the blessing of the Church for their relationships? At this stage it is an issue in our own hearts and heads, but pretty soon it becomes a person, a person knocking at the door like Cornelius, and we are called out of the refuge of abstraction to confront real human beings who are being victimised by those same abstractions. That has certainly been my own experience. What begins as abstract theorising, almost as an intellectual game, soon becomes flesh and blood that makes its challenge directly and won't let me escape into theory. 'Your theory, this abstraction you struggle with, is actually about *me*, and it is causing me to suffer. Your theology *hurts* me, gets me beaten up, sometimes killed: think about it!' Peter certainly thought about it, when confronted by Cornelius, but we know that he was not really converted, not really turned round inside, because he equivocated on a number of occasions, later on. Like many leaders he wanted to keep his options, or his avenues, open to both sides.

From our point of view, the thing to notice is that all of this is going on inside us all the time. We can all testify to moments of conversion, moments when the scales fell from our eyes and we *saw*, for the first time, how racist or sexist or homophobic we had been. We did not really admit it to ourselves, of course, but it showed itself in all sorts of ways, usually by our use of language, by the throw-away remark that's meant to be funny, but betrays deep prejudice or fear. When the moment of conversion comes, the moment we see what has been going on inside us, we use the language of revelation, the language of disclosure. William Temple claimed that scripture was the witness to the gradual revelation of the true nature of God to humanity. We can use that language within the world-view that suits our own contemporary way of putting things. Yeats was right:

> '*Now that my ladder's gone*
> *I must lie down where all the ladders start*
> *In the foul rag and bone shop of the heart.*'[3]

231

Footnotes

[1] Brenda Maddox, *George's Ghosts,* Picador, London, 1999, pp.127,128

[2] Friedrich Nietzsche, *The Genealogy of Morals,* third essay, section 15,
 The Basic Writings of Nietzsche, The Modern Library, New York, 1992, p.563

[3] WB Yeats, *The Circus Animals' Desertion,* The Poems, Everyman,
 London. 1998, p.394

Preaching

Alastair Haggart

Of all clerical activities, preaching is perhaps the one held in lowest esteem. "Oh for goodness sake don't preach at me!" or "Stop sermonising". It's not new – there have in the past been times and places in which preaching was disesteemed. Some of you may know Browning's poem on Christmas Eve:

> '*I very soon had enough of it,*
> *the hot smell and the human noises*
> *and my neighbour's coat – the greasy cuff of it*
> *were a pebble-stone that a child's hand poises*
> *compared with the pig of lead-like pressure*
> *of the preaching man's immense stupidity*
> *as he poured his doctrine forth full measure*
> *to meet his audience's avidity.*
> *My gorge rose at the nonsense and stuff of it*
> *I flung out of the little chapel.*'

Well, we may not always react quite as violently as Browning, but perhaps we know how he felt. Unfortunately, preaching today encounters problems that didn't exist in an earlier age – the pre-media age. Wherever you go today, when you are travelling, in restaurants, your own home, so often there are unattended background noises of music or talk. We have become accustomed to this background of mostly ignorable sound, so that in church it requires a conscious effort to listen, to attend to what we are hearing. And this is true not only of preaching, of course, but of prayers in the service. So the demand on the preacher is greater and not less. He has got a greater competition to gain his audience's, his congregation's attention.

Some, including practising Christians, including even preachers, have given up. Sometimes there is an unexpressed collusion between preacher and congregation and they fall into a kind of cycle of deprivation. The preacher senses that these people are not prepared to be seriously engaged – all they look for in a sermon is brevity. If a preacher tells an interesting story that's a bonus. So the preacher thinks "Why should I bother, why should I spend time wrestling with a sermon?" The hungry sheep may look up but all they want is candy floss, so he doesn't bother – he just knocks up a few words. Then his congregation, when it hears the few words, is confirmed in its judgement – his sermons aren't worth listening to – just a lot of pious platitudes. So they switch off and long for the conclusion and the preacher senses this. His judgement is confirmed – preaching is a dead loss. And so the cycle of deprivation, and indeed of degradation, continues.

But it needn't be so. A preacher and his congregation can actively, deliberately, not *collude* together, but *covenant* together to enter into a cycle of affirmation. One of the most important duties of a preacher to his congregation is to preach about preaching – to reflect with his congregation what, before God in this act of worship, is supposed to be going on in the sermon. What does it mean when the preacher prefaces his sermons with the words "In the name of the Father and of the Son and of the Holy Spirit" or "May the words of my lips and the meditations of my heart be always acceptable in Thy sight"? And what does it mean when the congregation says "Amen" to that?

I have said that all too many congregations bring only one expectation to the sermon – that it should be brief. Let me say then something about sermon length – about the congregation's attention span. Clearly there are both external and internal constraints on a preacher as far as time is concerned. Perhaps, as in one congregation to which I ministered, the local bus service made it impossible for the service to begin before a certain time and made it essential that the service should end by a certain time. And then this external constraint, which was totally beyond our ability to alter, determined very largely how long the sermon should be, but not entirely. How are we going to use the time available? How much to hymns, prayers, notices and so on? Must the sermon time always be the first to be cut?

There was a very famous Church of Scotland preacher called Archie Craig and he used to say "Duration is a secondary consideration. A good sermon of thirty minutes may be just right, a bad sermon of three minutes is always far too long."

Sermons, quality, content, as well as duration, should be discussed by the preacher with his congregation and some initial agreement reached. I have myself known it happen that, as mutual expectations of quality between preacher and people rose, duration, given the external constraints if any, no longer was a problem.

But what is a sermon? A sermon is not a lecture. A sermon always takes place in a context of worship and one definition of a sermon is certainly worth thinking very seriously about. A sermon is breaking of the Word. As in the Eucharist or Holy Communion we break the bread, so in a sermon we break the Word. Preaching has a kind of sacramental quality about it. And just as we don't use special bread or wine in the Eucharist, but the ordinary bread and wine offered to God and blessed by the holy Spirit become more than their everyday physical reality, they become as well the means whereby Our Lord Jesus Christ himself enters into the most profound and personal relationship with us that we may ever more dwell in him and he in us; so in preaching we offer to God together the words of our lips and the meditations of our hearts and through the Holy Spirit they become the vehicle whereby human speech and human listening become the vehicle by which Jesus Christ himself speaks to us. Now I know this is a very high doctrine of preaching, but nothing less will do.

Preaching is a shared and joint activity of preacher and congregation, and one of the prayers that I used to use when I was a parish priest was quite simply "Oh God, the Holy Spirit, speak through me and hear in them". And when preacher and congregation realise that it is in this context that the sermon is taking place, then expectations cannot be other than high. And it is perhaps because the Old Testament prophets had this exalted understanding of their vocation to speak the Word of the Lord that they called it. 'The Burden' and came to their ministry as prophets with such reluctance.

We mustn't enter the pulpit too light-heartedly. We are not here to show off how clever we are or to enjoy and be flattered by our own rhetoric. Nor are we sitting in the pews to be entertained by rhetoric or amused by interesting stories. Preaching is an enormously demanding, corporate activity and unless that is recognised in both pulpit and pew there can be no true preaching. It doesn't mean we've got to be too solemn about it – pompous – but we have to take it very seriously indeed.

But given this understanding of what a sermon is, what are we going to preach about? Sunday after Sunday, year after year, even if, as now is mostly the case, many denominations offer us a two or three year Scripture lectionary with themes attached to each Sunday, and readings corresponding to the cycle of the Church's year.

We can of course be very high-handed and say, as Bishop Gore is alleged to have said when he was a Canon of Westminster "I preached in this pulpit on Easter Day last year. I have not in the interval changed by beliefs about the Resurrection, so I intend preaching the same sermon again this morning." There is of course no reason why we should not preach the same sermon twice, even to the same congregation. There's almost certainly, if there's this high level of expectation, far more in any one sermon than any congregation can take aboard in one hearing. So there is no reason why we should not preach the same sermon twice though perhaps we should not try to imitate Bishop Gore in doing it in successive years. But sometimes, even with lectionary themes, the preacher feels dry and at a loss for ideas for sermons, and so we must build up a reservoir of ideas appropriate to the congregation to whom we are preaching. Here the whole background of our reading, of our pastoral experience of what our parishioners, of what our fellow clergy say and do, of what we hear or see on radio or television, in fact our whole life experience, provides us with ideas and we will be delivered from that awful Saturday night feeling: "What on earth am I going to preach about tomorrow?" But you must jot down your ideas as they come – don't trust your memory. **The strongest memory is weaker than the weakest ink.**

And of course there are all kinds of sermons and all kinds of subjects. Some are straightforward scripture exegesis, leading to a better understanding of the bible, or a better understanding of some particular doctrine of the Christian faith. These are straight sermons of instruction. There are also sermons on prayer and spirituality, very frequently leading to the practice of prayer in the course of the sermon. Other sermons are on ethical issues or social or political issues, but not in too black and white a way. They are invitations to the congregation to consider with you particular understandings and interpretations of whatever you are preaching about. Remember that you may know more theology than your people do, but they may have a far more direct and responsible involvement in the world of affairs than you have. And sometimes sermons should be general introductions to issues to be studied in discussion groups later. The sermon is the most important general vehicle of communication of the Gospel , but it isn't the only vehicle and it's very important that we should see it as being supplemented in all kinds of ways, in groups and with the use of various forms of media communication that are available to us today.

And when we are preaching I think we ought to be aware of too many illustrations. The sermon can be enriched, made more interesting and elegant, if there is a sparing use of apt illustrations and stories, but how often has one endured a sermon which has been really a series of stories barely related to each other and hardly at all to the supposed theme of the non-existent sermon.

And then, if we are in a parish alone, how often should we preach? Well if you mean by preaching what I mean by preaching, then normally not twice on a Sunday to the same people. Was it not Bishop Kent who said, "If I preach twice on the Lord's Day I praise once." Not so many congregations nowadays, I fear, have both morning and evening Sunday services, so perhaps the question doesn't arise. But if it does, you can have a service at which there is a whole series of distinguished visiting preachers in absentia. Of course you tell your congregation – you explain what you're going to do – and you say "During Lent, our preachers at Evensong will be Bishop Steven Neill, Bishop John Taylor or the Reverend Kenneth Slack or Cardinal Basil Hume", and so on – and you work on excerpts from these people's writings. They don't need to be sermons – anything they've written which you find illuminating and which you think your people would find nourishing – and you work on the text until you know it intimately, when you can read it intelligently and interestingly to your congregation. Of course, if you don't work at it, and just read it from the book, then your people will be bored to death, and you do a great injustice to your visiting preacher. If you do work at it, and learn to communicate in your reading the minds of the writers, you may very well find, as I used to find, that people in the congregations will later ask if they could borrow the book you had been using, or if you could give them more information about the writer to enable them to get books by him or her for themselves for their own study.

And then of course behind all this you've got to pray your sermons, and you've got to teach your people to pray your sermons too. Preaching is a dead loss if it's just a human activity of speaking or hearing. You may entertain your audience but that in itself isn't preaching. St. Paul knew that and we'd better know it too. "Making supplication for all the saints and for me also," he says, "that utterance may be given me in opening my mouth boldly to proclaim the mystery of the Gospel." Making supplication for all the saints and for me also in order that the Gospel may be proclaimed.

Well now, how are we going to fulfil this ideal? First of all of course our speech must be heard. Even if what we say is very much worth hearing, if it isn't audible no-one is edified, nor God glorified. Just as in our public buildings and homes we are today used to higher temperatures and better lighting, so we are accustomed to modern amplicifation. But if this is true, in our churches it must be properly serviced and maintained. There is nothing worse than being a member of a congregation listening to a sermon which may be very, very good indeed, but the equipment is so poorly serviced that all you hear is booms and crackles and echoes. We must learn how to use modern techniques and modern technology in order to help us communicate clearly, and be easily heard and followed.

And then you may remember that it's not only important that we should have something to say, and say it in such a way that it is heard – we've got to remember too the people to whom we are speaking. I can remember at school being told by a Latin teacher that the verb *ducare*, to teach, takes a double *accusative*, so that if I am going to teach John Latin, I have not only got to know Latin, I have got to know John as well, otherwise what I say will either go straight over his head or be so simple that he won't be interested and engaged at all. I think the same is true of our congregations. We've got to preach to our people's condition. And this is where the preacher is also a pastor. He is not preaching to strangers, and this is where a visiting preacher really doesn't work. He may preach a very interesting sermon and tell you something that your local clergyman couldn't tell you, but it's not the same as regular preaching, because he doesn't really know intimately the condition of the people he's preaching to. And this is where of course pastoral visiting comes into its own, having an intimate knowledge of your congregation, sharing their lives, their hopes, their fears, their joys, their sorrows, birth, death, marriage and so on – you know them intimately and they know you, and you are preaching to them in a context of mutual respect. You are bound together by deep bonds of affection. And this of course transforms sermons. What you are saying is not generalised, it is particularised for your people, and you will find that as you go out among your people they will feed you with what they say, the kind of questions they ask, the kind of concerns they share with you - they will feed you with all kinds of sermon subjects. So as you go on in your ministry in that particular congregation your preaching

240

becomes more and more addressed to the condition of your people.

But of course the preacher must not only know John, know his congregation – he must know Latin, he must know something of the organised tradition of Christian faith and belief and practice, and so a Christian preacher, ordained or lay, man or woman, stipendiary or non-stipendiary must constantly be equipping himself to preach. It's a lifetime's job, gaining a deeper understanding of the scriptures and the Christian tradition, of the doctrine of our faith and of the moral and social applications of our faith to our world. If the preacher's mind is not, under the guidance of the Holy Spirit, always being quickened and refreshed and enriched, how can the congregation be other than bored with religious platitudes? So the preacher is always learning and always equipping himself for ministry.

And this has never been more important than today when Christian congregations mostly don't know the Scriptures or the fundamentals of the faith as they once did. We are living in a largely secular society and even in our schools our children are not getting the basics that they once got, and so if Christian people are going to be equipped to understand their faith then they must make a real endeavour to do so and they must be encouraged and enabled to do so by their clergymen. Here, of course, there is a great need for a preacher to be honest, facing frankly with his people the problems of faith in the 20th century.

In general talk like this I must be careful not to assume that my own understandings and interpretations and convictions about the interpretation of the scriptures or traditional doctrines of the faith in our creeds and so on are shared by all. What I am about to say now is probably the most important thing I can say to you, and I say it with every ounce of conviction that comes from a ministry in both England and Scotland of over 45 years. Of course there can be a claim to openness and honesty that justifies insensitivity and an immature desire to shock people, I'm not talking about that – but remember the people to whom you are preaching week by week are not strangers, nor is your sermon a lecture as I have said. You are speaking in the name of the God of truth to men and women whom you have come to know intimately – you know their condition. So don't fall into the trap of thinking that people who are not very well educated are stupid. I know I have ministered to lots of people who left school at a very early age – 14 or 15 – who were very intelligent indeed and who were very shy of speaking their thoughts, but this did not alter the fact that they were capable of thinking, that they were capable of trying to relate what they heard in church to what they read in their newspapers or heard on radio or television – they were people of the 20th century and they wanted to be Christians of the 20th century.

You know them, they know and trust you. So there is very little danger in being honest with them, in coming clean with them, that you will in fact shock them, because they will trust you. Well now, if you are honest with them, if you have taken them into your confidence, you will find that they will begin increasingly to come clean with you, especially the younger members of your congregation. They will come to you confident that you too share their questions, that you are to be trusted to listen to their doubts and perplexities, that you have no prefabricated answers. Let me illustrate. If you are preaching about or from the scriptures, do you tell them flatly what they have to think? Do you utter a stream of phrases like "The bible says..." or do you invite them to explore with you what, in the bible, belongs to a vanished culture and what to the everlasting Gospel? Do you help them to explore and discriminate between what is secondary transitory and what is enduring? Or if you are preaching about the creeds, do you silence wonder and questioning with phrases like "The Church teaches...." or do you try to share with them your own pilgrimage towards a spiritually strong and nourishing faith without pretending that the formulations of faith in the past are completely and literally authoritative for the present?

Let me read to you something which Professor Nicholas Lash of Cambridge said recently at a conference of Catholic clergy in Leeds. He was talking about preaching and this is what he said.

"In my experience Catholics who deeply disagree about everything else nearly always agree, and with some passion, about the poverty of preaching. There can be no more conclusive proof of the extent to which Catholic Christianity is not understood to be a ministry of the Word than our sermons. On this sad fact, two comments. In the first place, much Sunday preaching is infected with untruthfulness. I do not mean that preachers lie to, or deliberately mislead their congregations, but by and large I think that they simply do not much care what they say. How do I know this? Because good speech, apt and accurate and truthful speech about things that really matter to the speaker, calls for the labour of craftsmanship. With word carving, as with wood carving, the lack of such labour is not difficult to detect. And in the second place the language of too many sermons hovers in some no-man's land far from particular fact, event and need, born of collusion between, on the one hand an indolent biblical fundamentalism, and on the other, abstract evocation of feeling or equally abstract exhortation to virtue. What is missing is firstly the particular facts, ugly and beautiful, which surround us on every side; secondly the words that might enable us to interpret these facts in the light of the Gospel. It is amazing how seldom one feels at the end of the sermon that anything at all has been actually said".

Now that's a pretty damning condemnation. But I know what he means, and sometimes I know to my shame that I have contributed to what he is describing. There was a great Quaker New Testament scholar, H.J. Cadbury, who wrote many very large books, and one or two quite small ones. One of the small ones was called '*On the Perils of Modernising Jesus.*' Of using, for example, 20th century insights into crowd psychology to explain the feeding of the five thousand. The little boy's generosity with his fish and bread shamed the adults into sharing their picnics. Or the 20th century insights into psychosomatic mind/body interaction to explain healing miracles neither were, nor were told to be, interpreted like that. That is the peril of modernising Jesus and totally misreading the Scriptures. But there is another little book entitled '*On the Perils of Archaeising Ourselves*'. Must 20th century people pretend to be 1st century people before they can receive the Gospel? Can the Gospel not be preached to, and received by, children in a scientific age?

But we must listen not only to the producers. What do the consumers think? Let this modern schoolgirl speak to us, as she spoke in a television interview. She is a product of a secondary modern school. "I wouldn't say I don't believe in the existence of a supreme being, but I don't know how people can really believe that a being that made this universe so intricate, so unbelievable – how can people believe that such a being sent down a child who was crucified and then rose from the dead and went up to heaven in a cloud? You know, it's so crummy isn't it?"

Now in a sense this girl is very near the Kingdom of God. She has got this sense of wonder – she is at least astonished into incredulity by the Gospel. And how much better that is than to take it all for granted, as though God becoming man and dying and rising again was the most natural thing in the world; not something that stirs our astonishment, not something that makes us stop and wonder.

So it's not always the clergy's fault. Congregations often get the kind of preaching they desire and deserve and that is why we must train our people to expect great things. To outrage may be wrong, to shock may be good, to stimulate, even to provoke, may be healthy and necessary, but what is always and everywhere wrong, is to provide pap and call it preaching.

Acknowledgements

John Armson, Robin Barbour, Ronald Bowlby,
Ernest Brady, Bill Brockie, David Bruno, Kay Carmichael,
Neville Chamberlain, Sam Chisholm, Colin Cranston,
Philip Crosfield, Hugh Cross, Kathleen Dall, Colin Davey,
David Dennison, John and Eileen Ferguson,
Elizabeth Ferrar, Graham Forbes, Robin Forrest,
Kevin Franz, Bob Fyffe, Alison Garroway,
Rosemary Garrod, Malcolm Grant, Ivor Guild, Mary Haggart,
Bob Halliday, Brian Hardy, David Harvey, Leslie Houlden,
Lady June Aberdeen, Mother Janet of Whitby, David Jasper,
Mary Kinghorn, David Lawson, Robert Lightband,
Ted Luscombe, Ken MacAulay, Pat McBryde,
Alistair McFadyen, Hugh McIntosh,
Lord Mackay of Clashfern, Libby Macrae, Jim Mein,
Ian Michael, Philip Morgan, Gina Nankivell,
Michael Paternoster, Martin Reardon, Gordon Reid, George
and Libby Renwick, James Robertson,
Lewis Robertson, Patrick Rodger, Robert Runcie,
Elizabeth Salter, Bill Scott, David Shepherd,
Paul and Geraldine Singleton, Sister Ann Patricia,
C. Percy Smith, Wismoady Wahono, Terry Waite,
Roland Walls, Arthur and Roberta Walmsley, Ian Watt,
Alan Webster, Frank Weston, Norman Wickham,
Kenneth Woollcombe, Jim Wynn-Evans

248